𝔗𝔥𝔢 𝔑𝔢𝔴 𝔜𝔬𝔯𝔨 𝔗𝔦𝔪𝔢𝔰
BOOK OF
FLOWER
GARDENING

By the same author:

*The New York Times Book
of Vegetable Gardening*

*The New York Times Book of Indoor
and Outdoor Gardening Questions*
(Joan Lee Faust and Lisa Oldenburg, eds.)

*The New York Times Book
of House Plants*

The New York Times

BOOK OF FLOWER GARDENING

Joan Lee Faust

Illustrated by Barbara Scholey

Times
BOOKS

PHOTO CREDITS

Molly Adams, p. 31 (top)
Burpee Seeds, pp. 15, 16, 25, 27, 82
California Redwood Association, pp. 32 (bottom), 35
Denholm Seeds, p. 85
Goldsmith Seeds, Inc., pp. 2, 9
Gottscho-Schleisner, Inc., pp. 36, 227
Harris Seed Co., p. 26
H. D. Hudson Manufacturing Company, p. 97
The New York Times/Bruce Hosking, p. 243
The New York Times/Robert M. Klein, p. 239 (top)
Northrup King and Co., pp. 54, 55
Park Seed Co., pp. 24, 51, 62
Stokes Seeds, Inc., p. 67
George Taloumis, pp. 31 (bottom), 32 (top), 99, 215, 216, 219, 239 (bottom)

Color illustrations by Barbara Scholey

Published by TIMES BOOKS, a division of
Quadrangle/The New York Times Book Co., Inc.
Three Park Avenue, New York, N.Y. 10016

Published simultaneously in Canada by
Fitzhenry & Whiteside, Ltd., Toronto

Library of Congress Cataloging in Publication Data

Faust, Joan Lee.
  The New York Times book of flower gardening.

  Bibliography: p. 258
  Includes indexes.
  1. Flower gardening. 2. Annuals (Plants).
3. Perennials. I. New York Times. II. Title.
SB405.F37   635.9   79-51449
ISBN 0-8129-0857-0 (hardcover)
ISBN 0-8129-6317-2 (paper)

Manufactured in the United States of America

10 9 8 7 6 5 4 3 2

To Bea,
with love

contents

why grow flowers?
xi

1
behind the scenes:
how flowers grow
3

Flower Names *3*
Flower Groups *5*
Hybrids and Hybridists *7*
Perennial Introductions *12*
Cultivars and Triploids *13*
Seed Production *14*
Perennial Production *17*
Saving Your Own Seed *19*
All-America Selections *19*
Fleuroselect *22*

2
designing the
garden
23

Light *24*
Exposure *25*
Soil *25*
Climate *25*
Color *26*
Succession of Bloom *27*
The Flower Border *33*
Drawing the Plan *34*
The Critical Eye *38*
Planting Diagrams for Flower Borders *38*
Special Situations *46*

Starting Seedlings Indoors   *49*

Making a Choice   *51*

What a Seed Is   *53*

When to Start   *54*

Three Basics for Growth   *55*

Containers   *58*

Toughening Time   *62*

Under Lights   *63*

**3
all about
seedlings**
49

Soil Preparation   *65*

Natural Soil Improvers   *67*

Drainage   *68*

Fertilizer and pH   *68*

Planting   *69*

Tools   *73*

**4
soil preparation
and planting
techniques**
65

Spring Cleanup   *77*

Thinning   *78*

Pinching   *79*

Disbudding   *79*

Watering   *80*

Grooming   *81*

Midseason Feeding   *82*

Staking   *83*

Summer Mulches   *84*

Dividing   *87*

Stem Cuttings   *89*

Replacement   *90*

Flowers to Dry   *90*

Fall Cleanup   *92*

Winter Protection   *92*

Pests and Diseases   *93*

**5
keeping up
the garden**
76

the flowers
103

the annuals   *105*
the perennials   *157*

6
shade
213

Deep Shade   *214*
Full Shade   *217*
Half Shade   *217*
Light Shade   *217*
What to Grow in Shade   *218*
Planting   *221*
The MFW System   *223*

7
planting in
special places
225

City Terrace   *225*
Cutting Garden   *231*
Hanging Planters   *234*
Pots and Tubs   *236*
Gardening by the Sea   *240*
Strawberry Jars   *242*
Vacation House   *245*
Window Boxes   *246*

8
flower lists and
useful information
249

All-America Award Winning Flower
Varieties in General Commerce   *249*
List of Flower Seed Varieties
Awarded by Fleuroselect   *253*
Sources for Flower Seeds and Plants   *253*
Cooperative Extension Services,
by State   *255*
Books to Read   *258*
English-Latin Index of Flowers   *260*
Latin-English Index of Flowers   *262*

index
267

why grow flowers?

Sitting where I do at the garden news desk of *The New York Times* would not seem a likely window on the garden world, but it does provide an expansive view. Flowers are coming back. Though they have not been very far away, a surging interest in reader mail indicates a trend.

There are other signs. Recently the vegetable garden was of primary interest. New homeowners discovered the flavor of home-grown tomatoes and lettuce free from agribusiness contaminants. Furthermore economic pressures may make the vegetable garden a necessity. Yet the extraordinary enthusiasm for vegetable gardening has leveled off. Flowers are now in the forefront and their sales curve is rising.

The knowledge of gardening focused by the home vegetable plot is encouraging homemakers to look for other opportunities to use their new skills. Fuel costs may shorten the family vacations to the lakes, beaches, mountains, and parks. More time will be spent around home. Homeowners also know that their real-estate investment is worth prime upkeep as a vital hedge against inflation.

From the commercial standpoint, mass production has finally caught up with annuals and perennials. Many kinds of flowers available only in exclusive quantity are being introduced through mass-marketing outlets at prices that appeal to the wallet.

The resurgent interest in flowers was underscored for me this past winter. A local group in my town asked if I would help them with a gardening program. It was a time when the seed catalogues were arriving in the mail and the weather outside was frightful. The obvious topic, we agreed, was how to plan and plant your vegetable garden.

A group of thirty or so women gathered, some novice gardeners, some experienced. There was to be a short talk followed by a question-and-answer period. The women listened, but not too intently. In fact a head or two nodded. I had the feeling I should get on with it and get to my final remarks.

The first question was on vegetable gardening. The second questioner wondered if she could ask something about growing flowers. The meeting came to life. A long evening was spent in a fascinating exchange of experiences growing flowers.

The audience had mastered the vegetable garden. Most of them had more or less got it down to a system and were planning to repeat the same exercise.

But the flower imperative is different. Flowers are grown for themselves.

A garden without flowers is unthinkable. The usual pink petunias by the patio or a border of plantain lilies and impatiens along the front walk may be enough to satisfy. The continuity of this flower display every year does have its comfort. But an adventurous spirit, a willingness to break the mold and try something new brings far greater excitement. The flowers are there to choose in every color, variety, size, and season of bloom. They can fit into the most intricate garden plans and designs. Some will grow with little care, while some flowers will challenge with their particular demands for soil, exposure, and tending.

This is the pleasure, the learning. Something happens to us when a new flower blossoms for the first time. It makes our day and from that moment the world is a wonderful place.

At the winter meeting my audience loved the opportunity to tell of their successes and failures, to ask others what flowers they grew in particular situations, and to learn where a favorite flower they dreamed of growing could be obtained.

This book is an opportunity to harness and direct such enthusiasm. I hope to encourage those who want to get started and learn how to grow flowers, and to show those with some experience how to take on new challenges. Flower growing can be one of our happiest lifetime pursuits. And so to you, these pages. Enjoy!

Joan Lee Faust

Greenwich, Connecticut
May 1979

𝔗𝔥𝔢 𝔑𝔢𝔴 𝔜𝔬𝔯𝔨 𝔗𝔦𝔪𝔢𝔰
BOOK OF
FLOWER
GARDENING

1. behind the scenes: how flowers grow

A flower is a blossom is a bloom. It is a debut, a coming out, the fulfillment of expectations. Yet there is so much more to what flowers are all about, a complex and fascinating behind-the-scenes story that is as much a part of anyone's flower garden as are a trowel and a watering can.

Flower Names

Few gardeners can get very far without bumping into Latin. Rather than be turned off by it, gardeners can learn much from the Latin names of plants. They are part of an international naming system, standard the world over. This system of nomenclature was developed by Latin-educated scholars in medieval times. At first the Latin names for plants were long series of words with assorted adjectives. A flower had as many as four or five Latin words in its name.

Gardeners will be forever indebted to Carolus Linnaeus (Carl von Linné), the Swedish scholar and botanist, who spent the greater part of his life (1707–78) straightening out the chaos in the classification of plants and animals to a simple binomial system. He not only clarified the nomenclature but named many plants. He even included one for himself, twinflower, a delicate wildling he first saw in Lapland, which is known as *Linnaea borealis*. Linnaeus' monumental efforts have withstood the test of centuries and the binomial system is now the scientific language used for all organisms.

The first word of the Latin binomial is the genus to which a plant belongs. Most properly, it should always be capitalized. The second word following is the specific name that says something about the particular plant: how it grows, where it was found, or perhaps who it was named for. It is written with a lowercase letter, as in *Viola tricolor*. This Latin binomial identifies the wild flower johnny-jump-up. *Viola* places it in the Violet genus, while *tricolor* describes the three colors of the flower. It is one of the parents of the modern-day pansy.

If you learn the Latin names you will broaden your knowledge of plants considerably. Specific names are often adjectives, as in *procumbens*, meaning "prostrate," *praecox*, meaning "very early," *sylvaticus*, meaning "of the woodland." So much of our own language is rooted in Latin that many meanings are obvious, such as: *lancifolius*, lance-leaved; *discolor*, two colors; *vernalis*, spring flowering. With practice, the Latin terminology can become one of your gardening tools. The system of Latin nomenclature for plants is governed by an international body which meets every five years to review and revise as it deems necessary.

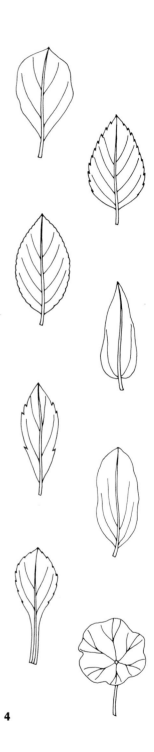

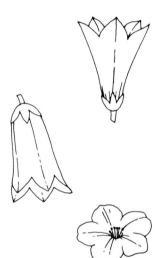

Flower Groups

Flowers belong in three groups. The two major ones are annuals and perennials, with biennials in between.

Annuals live for one year. They are planted outdoors at the start of the gardening season, flower, and usually keep blooming all summer. When the days shorten in fall, annuals start to taper off. Some set seed, others flower until frost kills them.

Some annuals are better started from seed indoors in late February or early March, either because they have very fine seed or are slow growers and need more time to reach flowering stage. Among these are petunias, snapdragon, and coleus. Unless these annuals have the head start indoors, they will not blossom until late in summer. If you don't have space to start these annuals indoors, there are plenty of commercial greenhouse growers who do and you can buy their started plants at garden shops in spring.

Other annuals are so easy to start from seed, you can plant them directly outdoors when the ground is suitable. They will flower quickly in time for you to enjoy them all summer. Among these are the favorites zinnias and marigolds. But all annuals will finish their growing at the end of the season.

Sometimes annuals "reseed" themselves with their own seed. When you are cleaning up the garden in spring, you might find some of these stray seedlings that wintered through if the ground was well mulched. Count them as mixed blessings. You might not want them as "repeats," so just pull them up.

Perennials are what the word means, they go on practically forever—most of them. The

5

perennials are herbaceous plants, that is, their leaves and stems are green and succulent, not woody. Their tops die down in autumn. These withered stems and leaves you can cut away in fall cleanup. But the roots, rhizomes or tubers, remain alive in the ground and survive the winter. New growth will start from them again in spring. As the years go by, perennials become thick and overcrowded. Many need frequent dividing or thinning out.

When you grow perennials, you usually start with plants or sometimes roots with sprouts, as with peonies and iris. These may be seedlings raised and sold by a nursery or cuttings that the nursery has rooted from either roots or stems. The newest type of perennial propagation is tissue culture, or "test-tube" growing, a highly specialized method carried out under sanitary laboratory conditions.

Some perennials you will be able to start yourself from seed available from catalogues. The important point to make here is that the seed must be of good fresh quality. And you will have to follow the precise instructions for each kind of perennial seed, for some need to be stratified or chilled for a period of time before they will germinate.

Biennials are in between annuals and perennials. They are two-year plants, that is, they require two years to fulfill themselves. Most of them you can start from seed yourself. They will grow the first year into strong, sturdy plants, but will not flower. The top will die down but the roots will live through the winter, just like those of perennials. The next year the biennial will flower, but then it will die after flowering. Some biennials set their own seed readily, however, and reseed themselves in place. These volunteers seem to be "perennials." Among them are foxglove and

The parts of a flower

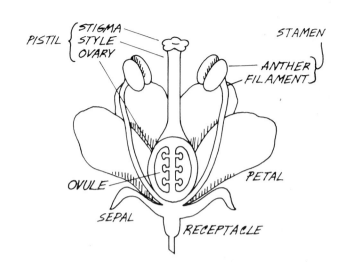

PISTIL { STIGMA / STYLE / OVARY }   STAMEN

ANTHER } FILAMENT }

OVULE

PETAL

SEPAL

RECEPTACLE

hollyhock. Two other popular biennials are Canterbury bells and sweet william.

The fact that a plant is an annual or a perennial has no bearing on the shape of its leaves. Some resemble lances or spoons and are round, while others are fat and wide. Some leaves have hairy surfaces smooth as a lamb's ear or rough like a cat's tongue. The flowers can be many shapes—bells, stars, cups, spikes, tassels, or hoods (as shown on p. 5).

Hybrids and Hybridists

Although a gardener grows annuals and perennials for flowers, the plants themselves have another goal: seed. The flower is the first step to the "fruit" or seedpod, and it is nature's intent to complete a life cycle and produce seed. Gardeners prevent this by cutting off old flowers and so prolong the display.

Professional flower growers let nature take its course and allow seed to develop. Without the work of these hybridists the flower garden would be very mediocre indeed. The

7

keenest work in hybridizing has been mainly in the production of annual flower seed. The industry is putting its money where the mass market is. Perennial flower seed production and hybridizing work goes on, but on a much smaller scale, since most perennials are propagated vegetatively by cuttings.

The organized breeding of annuals got a boost when hybridists began to work with petunias. Formerly varieties of petunias were maintained from year to year by rooted cuttings, an expensive and limited process, since those grown from seed were hit or miss. The seedlings were not of uniform size and the flower colors varied.

The ancestors of all modern-day petunias were two species sent to Europe from Argentina by a nineteenth-century French botanist named Petun. At first the flower had limited appeal in private and botanical gardens. By the latter part of the century, Mrs. Theodore Shepherd began breeding petunias in Ventura, California. She developed both single and double kinds with huge flowers that became known as California Giants.

By the 1930s petunia breeding intensified as selection and inbreeding techniques developed. Ernest Benary, a Germany hybridist, introduced an Erfurt Strain named for his town. These were grandiflora petunias, large-flowered with plain or fringed edges. A big leap forward came when T. Sakata, the remarkable Japanese hybridist, introduced his grandiflora double petunias. These were the first so-called F_1 hybrid flower seeds. But it was not until 1953 that the F_1 explosion for the production of annual flower seed took place in the United States. Charles L. Weddle, a Colorado hybridist, introduced Comanche, a bright red multiflora F_1 petunia. Although Comanche was in-

Breeding of hybrid petunias at the Goldsmith Seeds, Inc. greenhouses in Gilroy, California starts when the flower is partially open (2). Petals are split open (3) to reveal unripe anthers which are removed with a pair of tweezers (4). Close-up of the emasculated flower now ready for pollen (5). The pollen of the male parent (6) is allowed to ripen, removed (7) and applied to the female seed parent (8). This is the hybrid "crossing." The stigma of the petunia with pollen attached (9) and the final stage, the seed pod (10).

8

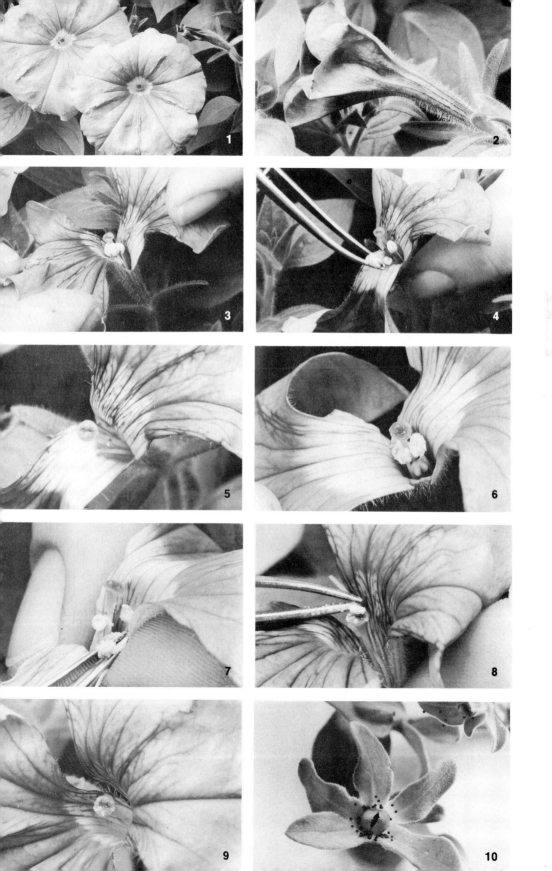

troduced twenty-six years ago, it remains a standard today.

The F_1 hybrids changed the annual flower seed business from a seed-rack/mail-order packet business to a huge mass-marketing system known as the bedding plant industry. This is the network of wholesalers who buy volumes of seed and grow the young annual seedlings or transplants for the spring garden market. These growers know that the newer hybrids will have the inbred quality control the home gardener desires. Current estimates consider that there are 12,000 growers in the bedding plant industry nearing $200 million annually.

You can also buy the seed of annual F_1 hybrid flowers either from seed racks or order them from the catalogues. They are all clearly indicated and the prices per packet are usually a little higher. Seed for only a few F_1 hybrid perennials is available, in particular the columbine Spring Song and several violas.

The "F_1" is a scientist's notation that means the first filial generation. A hybrid can occur in nature when two species cross-pollinate each other. An F_1 hybrid is different. It is a cross planned to blend the characteristics of two carefully developed inbred parents. The seed resulting from this cross will produce the F_1 hybrid plant. The mature annuals will look alike. Flowers will be the same color and the plants will be vigorous and uniform in size. What is more, as the breeding of this F_1 hybrid technique advances, geneticists include other beneficial qualities such as disease resistance, more flowers, earlier flowers, and better foliage.

Once established, inbred parents, or "lines" as the plant breeders call them, are carefully maintained. They are self-pollinated to control their uniformity and characteristics. There are some annuals and perennials that do not need the benefit of the F_1 hybrid vigor and are grown as inbred lines in commercial seed production and marketed this way. This is true particularly for the annuals alyssum, aster, celosia, and verbena, and the perennial hybrids such as the Russell lupines and numerous delphinium strains.

To achieve an F_1 hybrid petunia the two inbred parent lines are crossed. One inbred is designated as the pollen or male parent, while the other is the seed or female parent. In the early days of F_1 hybrid seed production, this crossing was done by hand, and still is for some seed crops such as petunia. The pollen of the seed parent is removed (emasculated) before it ripens and the pollen from the male parent is brushed upon the ripe stigma of the female flower.

In time the tiny seedpod forms and swells until the seed matures. Initially these pods were picked by hand and cleaned. This was a tedious process, and particularly so for petunia seed, which is very small, approximately 265,-000 seeds to an ounce.

A major step in commercial flower-seed production came with the development of pollen-sterile lines for seed parents. These lines eliminated the need to emasculate each flower by hand and permitted open field cultivation of F_1 hybrids. Pollen-sterile lines for field production have been established for petunias, zinnias, and snapdragons. Advances in the production of F_1 hybrids have moved along at such a galloping pace that gardeners will now find catalogues listing them for ageratum, begonia, chrysanthemum, dianthus, geranium, impatiens, marigold, pansy, salvia, snapdragon, and zinnia.

The advent of F_1 hybrids by no means downgrades the excellent annual and perennial flowers available that are not F_1 hybrids. Many flowers have such superior inherent qualities that they do not need the expense of F_1 hybrid breeding. F_1 hybrids are developed only for those annual and perennial flowers that can be improved by the process.

Perennial Introductions

Since so many perennial nurseries do their own propagating, they must also maintain the races of perennials in highest quality in their production fields. The growers are always on the alert for new or better plants in their own stock collections. While checking fields to maintain the standard of quality, a chance mutant or surprise seedling has often led to a new introdution. A few nurseries now have hybridizers on their staff. And all nurserymen visit back and forth with each other, both in this country and in Europe, to keep abreast of new introductions, color breaks, and hybrids.

As you study perennial nursery catalogues, the international aspect of perennial breeding becomes apparent. Fascinating histories could be written for many perennials.

The ancestry of peonies and chrysanthemums dates back to ancient China and Japan. Some of the prize perennials are domesticated wild flowers of other lands. Many of the modern perennials trace their beginnings to fine breeding work done in many of England's famous nurseries. Blackmore and Langdon are synonymous with delphiniums and tuberous begonias. Ingwerson Nursery has developed scores of outstanding perennials, particularly those such as yarrow. Individuals have given their names to outstanding perennials. A Yorkshireman, George Russell, will forever be remembered for his Russell lupines. The Swiss nurseryman Carl Frikart named the lovely *Aster Frikarti*. And in America, Alex Cummings commemorated his famous Bristol Nursery in Connecticut with his hybrids, including the baby's breath, Bristol Fairy.

Cultivars and Triploids

A useful new word was recently spawned in the horticultural world: "cultivar." It is an attempt to be more precise when defining plants that are cultivated as opposed to those variants that occur in nature. In the true botanical sense, a variety is a subdivision of a species.

But somehow the professionals felt that a better word was needed when referring to a race or variety that has horticultural importance. So the word "cultivar" has been coined. We used to say that Comanche was a variety of petunia, but now it is considered more accurate to say Comanche is a cultivar of petunia.

Seed-catalogue shoppers will come across another tongue-twister in the description of flowers, "triploid hybrid," the result of a diploid-tetraploid cross. A diploid is a normal plant with the usual number of chromosomes, the gene carriers for transmitting plant characteristics. The tetraploid is a flower treated with colchicine, which increases the number of chromosomes to make the flowers larger and the plants more vigorous. When the diploid and the tetraploid are crossed, the result is a triploid with a triple set of chromosomes. The purpose of this cross is to achieve a particularly long season of flowering. The triploid is sterile, incapable of producing seed, and so it flowers continuously from early summer to frost. The Nugget Hybrid marigolds developed by the Burpee Seed Company are one of the finest examples. These triploid hybrids, which Burpee calls marigold mules, are cunning dwarf plants which flower continuously all summer.

Seed Production

Just as California's Imperial Valley is considered the produce basket of the country, so is the Lompoc Valley north of Santa Barbara the flower-seed basket of the country, even the world. The broad, flat valley is ideal for growing both annual and some perennial flower seed. It casts a magic spell when seen from the hillsides above, a Paul Bunyan quilt come true. The assorted squares, oblongs, and patches of thousands of flowers in full bloom in every imaginable color make an unforgettable sight. The colors stretch as far as the eye can see, with tiny ribbons or roads and small buildings punctuating the pattern.

The Lompoc Valley's climate is ideal. Fields are irrigated during the dry growing season while the flowers are developing and maturing. The seed ripens quickly and dries fast. Mechanical harvesters go in and thresh or vacuum the seed quickly; then it is cleaned and stored for shipment.

Most of the seed sold by retail seed catalogues and from packets is grown under contract in these enormous production fields. The retail companies do their own individual packing. Some retailers grow a portion of their own seed, but not significant amounts. The

Burpee's Nugget marigold is a sterile triploid hybrid.

Advances in flower breeding have introduced shaggy, cactus-flowered and dahlialike zinnias.

14

A field of asters
being grown for seed
at Burpee's Floradale
Farm in Lompoc,
California.

Park Seed Company, considered the largest retail mail-order seed company in the country with distribution of eleven million catalogues, grows only two percent of its own seed. The rest is grown under contract all over the world—in Australia, Japan, India, Africa, and Israel as well as in the United States.

Perennial Production

The mass propagation of perennials for retail sale is more complicated. The range of perennials available for home gardens is far more extensive than the assortment of annuals. For perennials may have many species and races within the species. Many of them are wild flowers from other parts of the world. Columbines have seventy species for example, but only a dozen or so are grown.

Purchase of perennial plants is more trustworthy on a regional basis from local nurseries. Plants that are shipped long distances often suffer badly from the mail system. Most mail-order perennial nurseries that do ship keep plants until they are at least a year old so they can withstand the rigors of the postal service. Their bare roots are wrapped in sphagnum moss to prevent desiccation. Since the shipping season for many nurseries is in the early spring months when the ground is too wet to dig or is even still frozen, the plants are dug in fall and held over in cold storage until spring. Upon arrival the plants appear to have little semblance of life, but they are alive. If the planting instructions provided by the nursery are carefully followed, particularly with regard to watering plants in after setting them out, all should grow well.

17

Many perennial nurseries never ship plants and sell only on a cash-and-carry basis or deliver locally. Small nurseries and garden centers that do not have the propagating and growing space or trained staff buy from regional wholesalers.

The perennial nurseryman is doing some form of plant propagation, growing, or potting twelve months of the year. Perennials are sold in all stages of development: seedlings, root cuttings, stem cuttings.

Another advance that has helped to increase the new surge in perennial popularity is container growing. A great number of nurseries now pot their young perennials in individual pots and "hold" them to salable size in cool greenhouses over the fall and winter months. They leaf out nicely for spring sales, when the bulk of them are sold. But because they are growing in individual containers, these perennials can just as easily be bought and planted in summer or fall when there is less chance of their roots being disturbed.

A few nurseries now ship young container plants, either seedlings or rooted cuttings, four to five months old. They are packaged in six-pack pots, one inch square and two inches deep, and sold as what the nursery trade calls "liners." The younger plants are less expensive to buy but take longer to mature. The responsibility and time-expense become the buyer's concern rather than the nursery's.

These liners are an inexpensive way to start a brand new perennial garden. They are also economical if a great number of perennials are needed for a mass planting. They require patience to wait out their maturing, as many may not flower until their second year.

Saving Your Own Seed

Should gardeners save their own seed? No, for with all the complicated parents that flowers have these days, any seed from your own flower borders are bound to be disappointing. The chances are that a great deal of the seed will not germinate, and if it does, the offspring may be quite different from the lovely flowers their parents produced.

All-America Selections

As progressive steps developed in flower-seed production and a proliferation of cultivars appeared, the seed industry began to see the need for some kind of evaluation system. They wanted to test how their annual introductions fared in other parts of the country and how they compared with those of their competitors. They also wanted to have display grounds where they could observe the new and improved varieties.

The result was the All-America Selections (AAS), an organization formed in 1932. Initially the group had a dozen commercial plant breeders and university professors. They monitored sample plantings in their area where the new seed-grown plants were received for review. These sample plantings became known as trial gardens. The vast majority of the entries are annuals, but sometimes there are perennials. Currently there are over fifty-five trial gardens located in the United States and in Canada, where both new flowers and new vegetables, grown from seed, are reviewed. Each trial garden has an officially designated judge for the entries. Many of these

The trial gardens
at Pennsylvania
State University
are a gathering
point for flower
breeders from
around the world
during the summer
months.

trial gardens are located on the grounds of seed company home offices and they are usually open to the public.

The entries in the AAS trial gardens are submitted by seed companies or governmental agencies and occasionally by private breeders. For comparison, they are grown next to a cultivar already in commerce. The AAS judge critiques these entries from observations made during various stages of the growing season. The scores are tabulated in the AAS headquarters in Los Altos, California.

Bronze, silver, and gold AAS can be earned. There have been as many as ten winners in one year, but there usually are fewer. Announcements are made through the media. Financial support for the organization comes from a modest assessment on the sales of winners.

An AAS Award is a badge of honor for the seedsman who earns it and an assurance for the gardener who buys it that the winner is the best in its class. All AAS winners are identified by the red-and-white-and-blue shield which is printed both in seed catalogues and on the seed packet.

The publicity granted these prize winners also provides hybridizers and producers with incentive to develop new entries. The financial investment required for any novelty is considerable, both for the initial time and effort spent in breeding and for the cost of marketable seed production.

There are 129 AAS Award flower cultivars currently available. Annuals are by far the largest category. Zinnias are the most frequently awarded flower, with twenty-five of them prizewinners, marigolds are next with nineteen, followed by a dozen petunias. The others are a grand assortment of flowers running literally from A to Z. The few perennials include a columbine, a delphinium, and a foxglove (see chapter 8 for the full list).

Fleuroselect

Although a generous amount of flower breeding is done in the United States, it would be remiss to omit the extensive work being done in The Netherlands, Japan, Germany, England, and France. American seed companies also have breeding fields in Costa Rica.

Flower seed breeders and merchants throughout Europe started an evaluation organization in 1970. Called Fleuroselect (Fleur for flowers and euro for Europe), it is head-quartered in The Hague. It is similar to AAS in sponsoring trial grounds in nearly every country in Western Europe and makes awards based on reports of the judges. Quite often American flower novelties are entered in these trials and vice versa. Occasionally, an outstanding flower will win both an AAS Award and Fleuroselect. To date four annuals have been so honored: Dahlia Redskin (1975); Marigold Showboat (1974); Zinnias Cherry Ruffles and Yellow Ruffles (1978). A complete list of all Fleuroselect awards is on page 253.

2. designing the garden

Blessed are those who have both the talent to design a beautiful garden and the skill to grow plants well. One quality enriches the other.

The delightful part of designing a garden is that the plants are alive and flexible. They can be moved, discarded, or increased as you please. A flower garden is not set in cement, you are not drawing architectural plans. If the garden looks unattractive after completion, you can revise it. This is far less traumatic than tearing out a badly designed kitchen and starting over again.

Rare is the garden plan that makes a perfect score the first year. This is part of the fun. The pinks may not be as pale as remembered or as described in the catalogue, or a delightful low edging plant may end up being taller than the plant behind it.

A major handicap for designers is that much of a garden plan has to be done from memory. No flower garden can ever be designed on location with plants in full bloom ready to move into place. Plants bloom at different seasons, and they come from all kinds of sources. Good design depends on individual skills, plant descriptions gleaned from books and catalogues, past experience, and some cultural knowledge. Most flower gardens are planned in spare hours, during long, cosy winter evenings by the fire, or between car errands such as running the children to school, team practice, and music lessons; or while perusing catalogues. Wise gardeners make notes while visiting friends who have gardens or when viewing impressive nursery gardens, and these help immeasurably when you're on your own. Most of all you must have a generous and tolerant spirit to design a flower garden.

Light

All the elements that will play a part in your flower garden must be brought to focus first. The prime determining factor will be the amount of light that will be available to the plants during the entire growing season. Remember, trees are leafless in early spring and what may seem like a lovely sunny space will be shaded in summer and fall. Shadows will also fall around a house or city terrace at different times of year and these will influence the degree of light and amount of sunshine available.

Light for plants is usually defined as full sun, half shade, and shade. A full-sun location would be a broad, open, exposed place that is treeless, such as a broad meadow, a large open terrace, or a wide lawn expanse where the sun touches the greater part of the day. At least six to seven hours of sunlight would be considered a full-sun location. Half shade would be about half of this with either morning or afternoon sun for part of the day. Shade is where the sun rarely touches but the light is bright enough to support some plant growth.

Hybrid dianthus

24

Deep shade is a limiting factor and would be the sort of location under the heavy foliage of maples and beeches where the ground beneath is always cool and damp. (Shade is discussed more fully in chapter 6.)

Exposure

Exposure is another way of describing air circulation or wind. Open city terraces are highly exposed and the wind factor is an essential consideration in planning any garden. A fenced city backyard has limited exposure and poor air circulation, while a large country acreage on a windy hill has extreme exposure. Sometimes windbreaks have to be installed where exposures are extreme, as on a beachfront.

Soil

Soil is a qualifying factor but it is not limiting. Any garden soil can be improved. But it must drain well. If the garden soil always has puddles after a rainstorm or if piles of snow hang in there in spring and melt away slowly, seek another location for the flower garden as there is no doubt a drainage problem and few are the flowers that will flourish.

Climate

Stick to the tried and trusted flowers that are known to be hardy (winter-proof) for your area. There is no sense in going exotic when such imports are known to be difficult for your climate zone.

If you ever have a question as to whether

Hybrid zinnias

or not a plant will survive in your region, you should be aware that the country has been divided into what are called hardiness zones. They are based on averages of winter temperatures and are excellent guides on the severity of weather in all parts of the United States. You will find the United States Department of Agriculture national hardiness zone map printed in many catalogues and garden books. Catalogue descriptions may note the climate zone for which the plant is hardy. A quick check for this information will save many disappointments if the plant is not suited for your region.

Variegated impatiens

Color

Color is what the flower garden is all about. But before picking favorite colors and putting them together in a willy-nilly patchwork, first consider all the colors on your property. The color of the house. What trees are around. Do they flower in spring with pink, white, red flowers? Are there shrubs around? Purple lilacs, orange or yellow azaleas, lavender rhododendrons, or pink and white laurel? Is there a gray slate terrace? A brick one?

Colors have degrees of intensity and these are important to consider. A dramatic statement can be made by intensifying colors. Generous use of white flowers around a white house with contrasts of green foliage can be magnificent.

Sometimes repeating a color over and over again in a continual thread through a border or along a path will soften lines and draw attention away from bad features in architecture. Subtle contrasts are often pleasing; lighter, softer shades blending with stronger shades of the same color are gentling. Flowers have designs in themselves that can be used en masse. Flowers with a dark outline on lighter-shaded petals are called "picotee" and have great appeal. So do their opposites, which are dark petals lined with a lighter color. Some of the begonia hybrids have these lovely contrasts. Or consider the bicolor petunias with their star-shaped white centers against a background of red or blue petals, or those with candy stripes.

Not to be overlooked are the colors and textures of foliage—the grasslike tufts of sea thrift, the handsome spires of iris, the softening grays of dusty miller, or the bizarre drama of coleus. Hosta may be bold green or variegated in green and white stripes, candytuft is dark green all year long, while the delicate fernlike texture of yarrow hints of summer meadows.

Choose the flower colors that please you, the colors you like. Place them boldly rather than in teasing touches, and then tie them all together with a continuous flow of color. This of course is easier said than done, but by drawing on perennials and annuals and not overlooking bulbs for spring, there is no reason for lack of a color at any time.

Succession of Bloom

The goal of continuous color is known in garden-planning jargon as "succession of bloom." Individual kinds of plants bloom at a particular time during the three growing seasons of spring, summer, and fall. The best approach is to select representatives from each of the bloom periods so that one color display follows another (see chart, pp. 28–29).

Dwarf calendula

BLOOMING

APRIL · MAY · JUNE

ANNUALS
- TOLERATE SHADE
- SUN
  - Pansy
  - African daisy
  - Heliotrope
  - Pincushion
  - Sweet pea
  - Crocus, daffodils, and tulips

PERENNIALS
- TOLERATE SHADE
  - Basket of gold, Candytuft, Leopards-bane, Primroses
  - Columbine
  - Bleeding heart
  - Forget-me-not, Speedwell, Lupine
  - F
  - Peony
- SUN
  - Bellflower, Orien
  - Beardtongue, Gas
  - Mountain
  - A
  - Rock cress
  - Avens, Pinks
  - Iris
  - Sea pink
  - Flax
  - Sneezeweed

PLAN

| JULY | AUGUST | SEPTEMBER | OCTOBER |

Begonia, Browallia, Coleus, Dusty miller
→

erfly flower, Cup flower, Flowering tobacco

To frost

Flossflower, Impatiens, Lobelia, Periwinkle, Sweet alyssum, Wishbone flower
→

helor buttons, Calendula, China aster, Four o'clock,
ve in a mist, Mignonette, Painted tongue, Phlox,
er, Pinks, Poppy, Swan River daisy, Tahoka daisy

Mexican sunflower, Spider flower, Strawflower, Sunflower

Cockscomb, Cosmos, Creeping zinnia, Dahlberg daisy, Dahlia, Gazania, Geranium,   To frost
Marigold, Moss rose, Nasturtium, Petunia, Salvia, Snapdragon, Stock, Verbena, Zinnia
→

Beebalm, Daylily

Balloon flower

Astilbe, Loosestrife

Plantain lily

Coralbells

pansy

e

Monkshood

phinium, Geranium

ppy

Tickseed, Yarrow

Blanket flower

Aster, Chrysanthemum

To frost

Baby's breath, Evening primrose,
False dragonhead, Hollyhock

Coneflower

Sunflower

Golden marguerite

Phlox

Stokes' aster

The bulk of spring's border color is provided by the hardy bulbs. The very earliest, such as snowdrops, will push up through lingering patches of snow in their eagerness to bloom. They are followed by crocus, daffodils, and finally tulips. The flowering limelight will also be shared at this time of year by the majority of the woodland wild flowers—trillium, hepatica, bloodroot. A few perennials join in— early phlox, candytuft, doronicum, forget-me-not, and bleeding heart.

The tulips share the landscape with the flowering trees—cherries, apples, dogwoods. They pave the way for iris, peonies, and Oriental poppies. Roses take over and flower in harmony with delphiniums and coreopsis, a splendid pair. Shasta daisies, daylilies, astilbes, and coneflowers join in.

By this time the annuals are in full flower and the splendor of annual and perennial bloom goes along until chrysanthemums and asters close out the flowering seasons.

Selections from these waves of flowers will provide something to look forward to in a garden from spring to fall, no matter how large or small the space.

All the flowers do not have to be planted in the same place to have this succession of bloom. The earliest spring flowers might be near the house because they are tiny and could be missed if planted too far out of sight. A border by the drive or front walk could be saved for summer annuals or chrysanthemums in fall. Perhaps pots of flowers around a pool or patio are where the big summer show should be. Window boxes provide another outlet and so do pots of flowers for the front door.

Don't be hesitant about using flowers in a lot of imaginative places. The home grounds

A late May border shows off coral bells and candytuft near a rustic fence.

Snapdragons, flossflower, phlox, and feverfew join in a midsummer display.

30

do not have to compete with a wholesale nursery in the quantity of flowering plants, but there are many nooks and crannies around a home garden where color can do wonders for brightening and accent.

The short walk to the front door of your home can be so much more welcoming with a planting of something as simple as geraniums set in a white bed of sweet alyssum. Or if that is too much to ask, how about two large clay pots by the door with a petunia in each one? When they fade, chrysanthemums can fill in just as nicely.

The Flower Border

The days of the huge perennial flower border have gone. Those magnificent displays, beautiful as they were in the heyday of estate gardens, required well-trained garden help to keep them going, or dedicated homeowners who devoted their lives to them.

The contemporary flower border should require only low maintenance. While no garden will tend itself, at least it can be designed for minimum care. And it need not consist exclusively of perennials. Perennials are included for that sense of continuity from year to year, but generous pockets of annuals are added for good summer color, along with bulbs for early spring display.

The flower border should not be a museum collection of plants, an assortment of everything that appeals from a catalogue. Select those plants that please you, that you enjoy for their color, fragrance, or beauty. The quality, not the quantity, is what counts. And don't be hesitant about repeating flowers in a border plan. That can also be part of its charm. The eye likes to flow from one color to another or from one leaf texture to another, but the pattern is restful if it has familiarity.

A straight line is not always the most pleasing. Sometimes a sweep, a curve, or a turn in the border can be more interesting, not an arbitrary curve or turn but one that follows a natural line in the landscape. If the property has a curve or angle, then why not have the flower border follow it or accent it? Sometimes a widening or narrowing at a certain point is just the element needed to make a planting of flowers intriguing.

And don't forget the element of elevation when planning a garden—consider the heights of plants, whether they are spires; bouffant billowing perennials; or fat, square, stocky annuals. Sometimes, while working with lines and squares on paper, the element of the third dimension—height—is overlooked. One of the most eloquent writers on gardening, the late Nan Fairbrother, reminds us of the pitfalls of paper planning in her book *The Nature of Landscape Design*. She tells us that we do too much planning on paper as if we were birds looking down on the scene, as if the landscape were a flat tray. We are ground-level animals who see in elevation, and we should plan with that perspective in mind.

Drawing the Plan

The practical way to plan a flower border, even a small one, is to draw it to scale on paper, ideally on graph paper. It is the only way to keep track of the space for planting and to figure accurately the number of plants that will fit into each space. Seed catalogues and nursery catalogues, books and packets will note

Daisies and snapdragons soften the lines of a wooden bench.

34

Hybrid geraniums and petunias pave a warm welcome to the door.

Hollyhocks and a picket fence are an old-fashioned team.

how far apart plants should be placed. For a good show no fewer than three perennials should be used, except for such huge plants as peonies, baby's breath, and gas plant, which can stand alone.

One advantage of the paper plan is that as you work out the color schemes, you can color in the various squares where the flowers are to be planted. This will help you to keep track of the colors and avoid any too obvious clashes.

You may want to rough out some temporary schemes on scratch paper first, before setting the final plan down on graph paper, but it should always be kept fairly close to scale. The location where the plants will go can be marked in circles. Once again, provide space for no less than three. Mark individuals with an x. These details will help you to total up cost and fill out order blanks when you are ready to purchase the plants. If the space of an early spring flower is to include room for color from a summer annual, this should also be indicated on the plan.

Two more important things to remember in working out the design diagram are to allow enough space between groups of plants for good air circulation and to allow enough space in between for your feet—at least twelve inches. You will have to get in to work around the plants, to weed, trim, water, and tend.

When planning for fall color, remember that the flowering season is often longer than you think, particularly if the weather is mild and frosts are delayed. One year in Connecticut, for example, begonias, ageratum, marigolds, lobelia, geraniums, alyssum, lantana, and remnants of petunias were still in bloom on October 20th.

The Critical Eye

Finally, when the garden is planned, planted, and flourishing, view it with a critical eye. If there are areas that please, you can purr and be satisfied. But if there are bloopers, gaps, and voids, either change them that season or make a note to do some revisions the following year. Victoria Sackville-West had a sense of this. She kept a magnificent garden at Sissinghurst Castle from 1930 to 1962, and she once wrote in her *Garden Book*: "One's best ideas seldom play up in practice to one's expectations, especially in gardening, where everything looks so well on paper and in the catalogues, but fails lamentably in fulfillment after you have tucked your plants into the soil. Still one hopes."

Remember that some flowers, particularly perennials, take a year or two to settle in and become themselves. Often another critical look the following year will demonstrate that you did better than you thought.

Make lavish use of the camera. It captures things that your eye does not always see. Pictures are excellent reference during the winter months when you are revamping or revising plans.

Keep records of what was planted, where it was obtained, and when. If you have to replace or reorder, you can do so easily without paging through reams of catalogues to find a particular species or favorite plant.

Planting Diagrams for Flower Borders

These planting diagrams suggest ways to arrange annuals or perennials or both for continual bloom. The combinations were selected for pleasing effects from flower colors, leaf textures and plant shapes—sprawling, spired, rounded, or tall. The borders can be made as long as desired simply by repeating the plan.

Annual border
for shade
3' x 6'

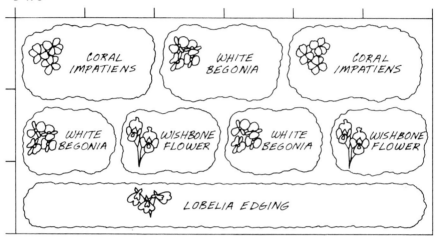

Blue lobelia, white begonias, and coral impatiens provide a long-blooming color scheme for shade.

Annual border
for sun
3' x 6'

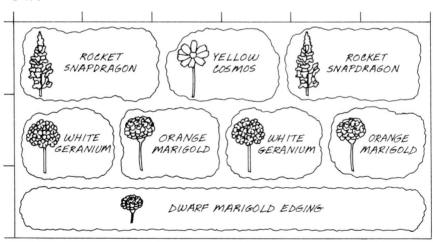

The mixed colors of tall snapdragons, yellow cosmos, and orange marigold are softened by white geraniums edged with dwarf marigolds.

Sunny border of annuals and perennials 5′ x 10′

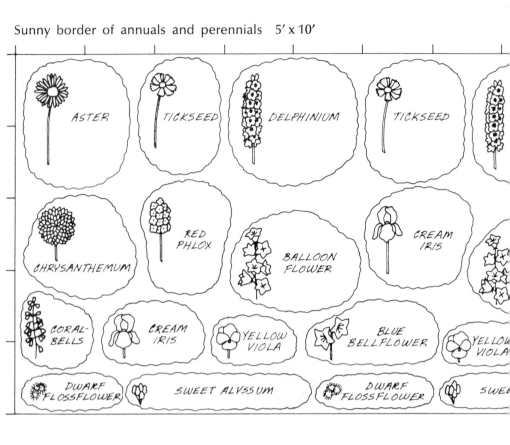

Annual border to plant from seed 4′ x 9′

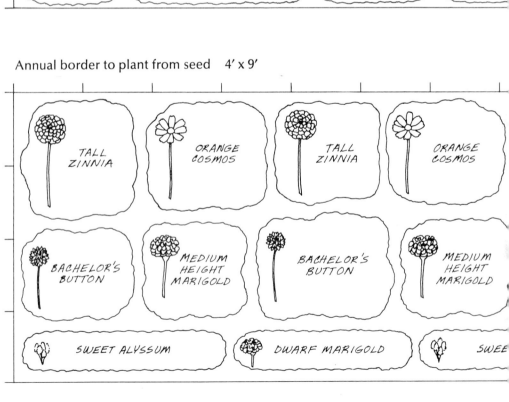

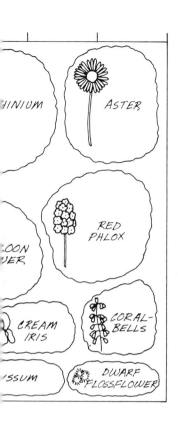

LINIUM   ASTER

OON
ER   RED
          PHLOX

CREAM   CORAL-
IRIS   BELLS

SSUM   DWARF
         FLOSSFLOWER

The interplay of flower colors in this mixed border of yellows, creams, reds, pinks, and blues lasts from spring to fall's chrysanthemums. Clusters of flower bulbs can be set out in fall for earlier spring color.

TALL
ZINNIA

BACHELOR'S
BUTTON

SSUM

All of the annual flowers shown can be seeded directly in the soil when the ground has been prepared. When the seed germinates, thin plants to one-half their height to allow room for proper growth.

41

Perennial border for shade

With extra attention of watering and light feeding, this blend of perennials will perform well in medium shade.

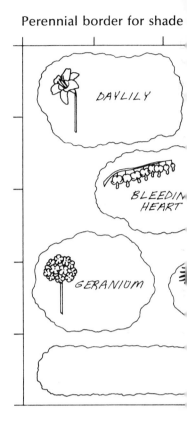

Low maintenance sunny

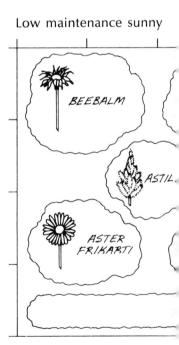

The daisylike rose-red blooms of beebalm, white Shasta daisy, and lavender-blue *Aster Frikarti* are spiced with the pastel plumes of astilbe and mixed colors of Rocket snapdragons. White petunias edged by lavender-blue flossflower unify the colors which will last most of the summer. Clusters of daffodils or tulips can be planted in fall for early spring color.

5′ x 10′

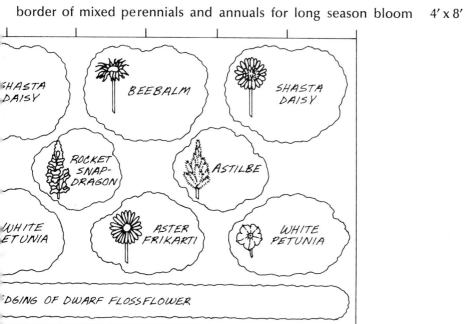

PEONY

FOXGLOVE

DAYLILY

MEDIUM HEIGHT DAYLILY

SPEEDWELL

BLEEDING HEART

JMBINE

ASTILBE

PRIMROSE

GERANIUM

CANDYTUFT EDGING

border of mixed perennials and annuals for long season bloom   4′ x 8′

SHASTA DAISY

BEEBALM

SHASTA DAISY

ROCKET SNAP-DRAGON

ASTILBE

WHITE PETUNIA

ASTER FRIKARTI

WHITE PETUNIA

EDGING OF DWARF FLOSSFLOWER

Two perennial borders for beginners
A 3' x 10' border
A 5' x 15' border

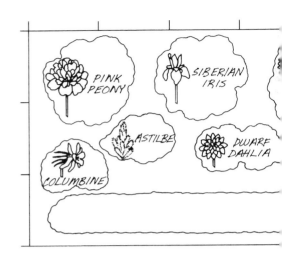

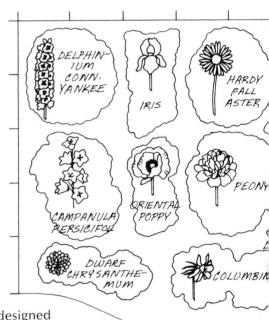

Both of these perennial borders were designed
by Elda Haring, a well-known gardener and
author, who has benefited from her own experiences with a 350-foot perennial border in
a New England garden.

44

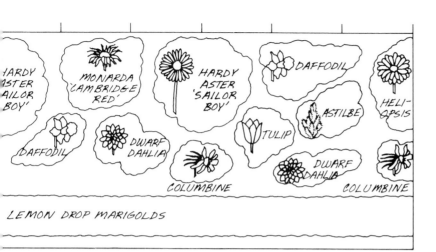

HARDY
ASTER
'SAILOR
BOY'

MONARDA
'CAMBRIDGE
RED'

HARDY
ASTER
'SAILOR
BOY'

DAFFODIL

HELI-
OPSIS

DAFFODIL

DWARF
DAHLIA

ASTILBE

TULIP

DWARF
DAHLIA

COLUMBINE

COLUMBINE

LEMON DROP MARIGOLDS

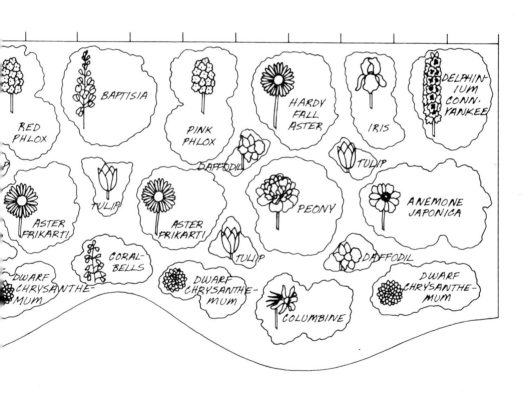

RED
PHLOX

BAPTISIA

PINK
PHLOX

HARDY
FALL
ASTER

IRIS

DELPHIN-
IUM
CONN.
YANKEE

DAFFODIL

TULIP

TULIP

ASTER
FRIKARTI

ASTER
FRIKARTI

PEONY

ANEMONE
JAPONICA

CORAL-
BELLS

TULIP

DAFFODIL

DWARF
CHRYSANTHE-
MUM

DWARF
CHRYSANTHE-
MUM

COLUMBINE

DWARF
CHRYSANTHE-
MUM

45

Special Situations

Hardy annuals to plant early in spring, or seed in fall for early spring bloom:

Bachelor buttons	Pansy
Calendula	Pincushion flower
Iceland poppy	Pinks
Larkspur	Shirley poppy
Love in a mist	Sweet alyssum

Tender annuals requiring warm soil before planting outdoors:

Ageratum	Nasturtium
Begonia	Periwinkle
Cockscomb	Petunia
Coleus	Salvia
Flowering tobacco	Verbena
Impatiens	Zinnia
Marigold	

Edging plants:

ANNUALS

Begonia (dwarf)	Moss rose
Browallia	Pansy
Creeping zinnia	Phlox (dwarf)
Cupflower	Pinks
English daisy	Sweet alyssum
Flossflower	Verbena (dwarf)
Impatiens (dwarf)	Wishbone flower
Lobelia	Zinnia (dwarf)
Marigold (dwarf)	

PERENNIALS

Astilbe	Iris (dwarf)
Bellflower (dwarf)	Pinks (dwarf)
Candytuft	Plantain lily (dwarf)
Coral bells	Phlox (dwarf)
Geranium	Speedwell (dwarf)

Flowers that need little care:

ANNUALS

Bachelor buttons	Marigold
Begonia	Spider flower
Geranium	Sweet alyssum
Impatiens	Zinnia

PERENNIALS

Baby's breath	Gas plant
Balloon flower	Peony
Beebalm	Plantain lily
Blanket flower	Sneezeweed
Bleeding heart	Speedwell
Coneflower	Sunflower
Daylily	Tickseed

Fragrant flowers:

ANNUALS

Flowering tobacco	Pinks
Heliotrope	Stock
Mignonette	Sweet alyssum
Nasturtium	Sweet pea
Petunia	Verbena

PERENNIALS

Beebalm	Peony
Evening primrose	Pinks
Iris	Plantain lily
Lavender	Primrose
Lupine	Viola

Perennials with a long flowering season:

Alkanet	Blanket flower
Astilbe	Coneflower
Beebalm	Coral bells
Bellflower	Flax

Geranium
Loosestrife
Phlox
Shasta daisy

Sunflower
Tickseed
Yarrow

Flowers for hot, dry, exposed locations:

ANNUALS

Bachelor buttons
Cockscomb
Cosmos
Creeping zinnia
Marigold

Moss rose
Nasturtium
Scarlet sage
Spider flower
Zinnia

PERENNIALS

Baby's breath
Basket of gold
Beebalm
Bellflower
Blanket flower
Coneflower
Coral bells

Flax
Lavender
Mountain bluet
Sunflower
Tickseed
Yarrow

Flowers for moist, damp locations:

ANNUALS

Calendula
Lobelia
Pinks

Sweet pea
Wishbone flower

PERENNIALS

Astilbe
Cardinal flower
Forget-me-not
Geranium
Leopards-bane

Loosestrife
Plantain lily
Primrose
Virginia bluebells

3. all about seedlings

Starting Seedlings Indoors

Newcomers to flower growing may wonder why anyone would even consider planting seed indoors before spring. After all, little trays of seedlings are very convenient to buy at any garden center, supermarket, or dime store. They are planted in commercial greenhouses early enough so the first flowers are usually in bloom. The colors are apparent and pleasing schemes can be worked out as you buy.

When the young seedlings are set in place, *voilà*, the garden is planted! For many this may be the best solution, particularly if the garden is small and just a few flowers are needed. This kind of instant gardening is ideal for those with a window box or two or for city gardeners with a small balcony or terrace.

But the flowers that you start from seed are rather special. Those who skip this are denying themselves a marvelous gardening experience. There is deep satisfaction in watching the little snippets of plants grow. And when they finally bloom, what can you do but rejoice?

Another point is that buying commercially started seedlings puts limits on flower garden possibilities. The selection of cultivars and the assortment from which you may choose was made by someone else, not you. The stock of bedding plants sold by most garden centers comes from wholesale growers who have the huge greenhouse ranges to supply this market. Their offerings are based on sales from the previous year. The flower (and vegetable/ herb) seedlings that sold well will be repeated. Those that didn't will be dropped or cut back, with some new items to fill in.

As this cycle repeats itself over the years, your garden is going to reflect the tastes of your neighbors. Of course, this is an exaggeration, but it does make a case for originality and for growing at least some of your flowers from seed.

Compare the huge assortment of annual and perennial seeds available from catalogues with what is available at most garden centers. Unless the retail source is an unusual one with custom growing space, there will not be the range of colors, or even plant sizes, available. A seed catalogue reaches a far greater number of customers and services a wider range of individual gardening tastes.

Few gardeners will have the space to grow all their flowers from seed, but a happy balance can be worked out between buying and sowing. Many perennials such as peonies, daylilies, and phlox should be started from nursery-grown plants. The seedlings to buy are the ones that are hardest to grow or that require a very early start indoors to reach garden-bloom size by summer. The flowers to start from seed are the different, unusual, and appealing ones that are rarely available at garden centers or those with particular colors that are hard to find. Sometimes a flower is interesting to grow just because it is said to be difficult—and you earn green-thumb points if you succeed.

Another reason for growing some annuals from seed is economics. Seedlings are not cheap, and when a huge number are needed for a long border or showy area along a drive or walk, space might be devoted to growing these plants indoors. Indoor gardening space is always at a premium for those who do not have greenhouses, a fluorescent light setup, or plenty of indoor plant space. Even then, house plants have to move over to make room.

Be warned, seedlings take up space. The tiny seed boxes or containers are only the beginning. Seedlings are transplanted to individual pots before they can be grown outdoors. Many people like to save steps and start the seedlings in individual pots, but there is no getting around the fact that seedlings need room.

Single marigold

Making a Choice

Here are the top dozen bedding plants that are sold nationwide as transplants (started seedlings). If some of them are in your plans, they might be the seedlings to consider buying. Particularly recommended for buying are petunias, coleus, geraniums, and begonias, which have almost powderlike seed that is difficult to start.

TOP BEDDING PLANTS

1. Petunia	7. Impatiens
2. Geranium	8. Ageratum
3. Marigold	9. Coleus
4. Pansy	10. Alyssum
5. Salvia	11. Zinnia
6. Begonia	12. Verbena

Marigold, alyssum, and zinnia, on the other hand, are so easy to start from seed that they can be planted directly in the garden as seed. The only reason for buying commercial seedlings is "instant bloom."

The annual plants not on the list are the ones to consider starting from seed. Studying catalogues can be a fascinating treasure hunt to find those flowers that will make the garden different. The descriptions of color, height, and habit of growing are always intriguing. A selection of the more unusual flowers may be just the trick to make the flower garden that much more appealing. The catalogue will indicate if the seed needs an early start indoors.

Many perennials are easy to start from seed, too, and a much cheaper way to acquire them if you grow your own. There are excellent choices in seed catalogues. Perennial seed can be planted indoors with annuals or you can wait until the outdoor planting season and sow perennial seed directly outdoors in a seedling nursery bed. Seed of some perennials is very short-lived and must be planted when fresh. The young perennials are transplanted to their permanent places in early fall or the next spring.

The following perennials are easy to start from seed:

Avens (*Geum*)
Bellflower (*Campanula*)
Blanket flower (*Gaillardia*)
Columbine (*Aquilegia*)
Coneflower (*Rudbeckia*)
Delphinium (*Delphinium*)
Evening primrose (*Oenothera*)
Flax (*Linum*)
Forget-me-not (*Myosotis*)
Foxglove (*Digitalis*)
Golden Marguerite (*Anthemis*)

52

Hollyhock (*Alcea*)
Lupine (*Lupinus*)
Mountain bluet (*Centaurea*)
Pinks (*Dianthus*)
Primroses (*Primula*)
Rock cress (*Arabis*)
Tickseed (*Coreopsis*)
Tufted pansy (*Viola*)

What a Seed Is

A seed is the flowering plant's means of self-perpetuation. In nature the seed is the means of replenishing the earth; grasses, weeds, trees, wild flowers, etc., renew themselves by their seed. Plants release them to grow in assorted ways. When the witch hazel's seedpod is ripe, it opens and shoots out twin seeds for a distance of nearly twenty feet from the parent shrub. Seeds of the Rocky Mountain lodgepole pine are packaged tightly in the cones. The cones cling to the trees for many years and remain closed until the heat of a forest fire splits them open to release the seed and renew the scorched earth. Dandelion seeds on the other hand, have an easy ride on a parachute to make a nuisance of themselves wherever they land.

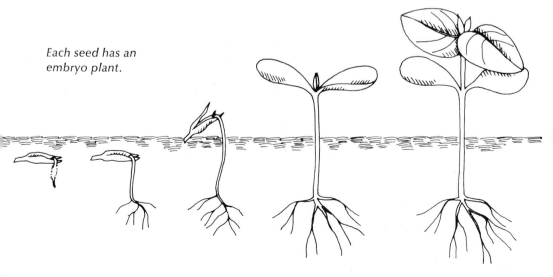

Each seed has an embryo plant.

Each seed contains an embryo plant which is surrounded by stored food so that it has nourishment to make the initial growth. This stored food is in the cotyledon. Grasses, corn, orchids, and lily seeds have one cotyledon, and are known as monocots. The majority of flowers have a pair of cotyledons around the embryo and are called dicots.

You may recall your high school biology classes when bean seeds (dicots) were grown between blotters as an illustration of how a seed grows. The two fat leaflike structures that spread apart to release the embryo plant are the cotyledons. They appear as "leaves" when they push above ground, but they are not leaves. The cotyledons are food-storage structures and will drop off. The next growths to appear will be the first pair of "true" leaves. Seed packets will often state, "Transplant seedlings when the second pair of true leaves appear." By this stage, the seedlings will be strong enough to withstand handling and root disturbance.

Larkspur

When to Start

Flower seeds may germinate in 5 or 6 days or in 3 or 4 weeks. Each kind of flower is set in its timing, and the number of days required will be important to know. This information will determine how soon you start the seed indoors. Seed catalogues and seed packets usually list the number of days for germination.

To determine when to sow, you'll have to do a little arithmetic. Add at least 4 to 6 weeks to the number of days needed for germination. The seedlings should be strong and actively growing when set outside. If started too

Salvia

Coleus

Cosmos

soon they become spindly and are too weak to take hold quickly.

No firm rules can be set because each gardener's indoor seed-growing environment will differ. Don't start too early and, of course, never too late. A range of 6 to 12 weeks before the outdoor planting date will accommodate most flower seed.

Three Basics for Growth

Flower seed needs three basics to grow: warmth; light; and an airy, well-drained planting mixture. Germinating seeds require a lot of inner strength to grow. Studies have shown that seventy-five percent of the food that seedlings produce during photosynthesis is used to grow.

For best germination, most flower seed should be kept warm, at room temperature, somewhere between 70 and 75 degrees. In severe cold weather, this means away from windowsills. Even though storm windows are tightly caulked, there is some cold-air seepage and it could be enough to delay seed starting. A work table near a warm sunny window is an ideal seed-starting location, as the tiny plants will need all the sun they can get. Or those who have space for fluorescent lamp setups may like to follow this method (discussed on p. 63).

As soon as seedlings germinate, they will grow better if the temperature is cooler, 60 to 70 degrees during the day, with a drop at night to 55 degrees. Few indoor growing spaces can be kept that precise, however.

The value of sunlight for growing seedlings —any plants—is well known. Sun is the catalyst that makes the seedlings grow. It is the go-power for the process of photosynthesis by which green plants can manufacture their own food.

The value of light for seed germination is of more recent knowledge. Some seeds need light to germinate. This seed is placed on top of the planting mixture and not covered. Other seed not requiring light to germinate is covered lightly—usually to the depth of the seed —with the planting mixture.

The following is a list of the annual and perennial seeds that require light to germinate. They are sown on top of the planting medium and the container in which they are planted should not be covered.

ANNUALS

Begonia	Impatiens
Browallia	Lobelia
Coleus	Petunia
Dusty miller	Salvia
Flossflower	Snapdragon
Flowering tobacco	Strawflower

PERENNIALS

Balloon flower	Rock cress
Columbine	Penstemon
Coral bells	Primrose
Foxglove	Yarrow

The planting mixture for seedlings must be lightweight and airy so roots can wiggle through it and can be easily separated at transplanting time. The roots must also have aeration to grow properly. A seed planting mix must be sterile. A subtle fungus disease, which lives in soil, can destroy a tray of seedlings overnight. Called damping-off, it chokes the seedlings at the soil line and topples them.

Sterile mixes bypass this problem, but the containers in which the seeds are planted must also be clean and sterile.

An assortment of seed planting mixes is available from garden centers and through mail-order catalogues. They come in several-quart to several-bushel sizes and are handy to use. These mixtures are the outcome of research for the bedding plant industry and are made of several formulas. One of the most popular is a blend of peat moss, vermiculite, and perlite. Some gardeners who have grown their own seed successfully prefer to use milled sphagnum moss rather than peat moss. Most packaged mixes contain some water-soluble nutrients; however, some do not. This is important to observe on the label, for it will determine how you maintain the seedlings after they start to grow.

Peat moss is decomposed organic material from bogs. Although many grasses such as sedges and reeds are derivatives of peat, the highest-quality peat moss for seed starting comes from sphagnum moss bogs. It holds moisture better and is not as far decomposed as the other peats. The sphagnum moss used for packing perennials and annuals for shipping is the parent material of peat moss. It is sieved or milled to break it into the fine particles which can be used as seed-starting material. Because of its light texture, it is better mixed with heavier substances such as vermiculite and perlite.

Vermiculite is a mineral made by heating mica to 1400 degrees. The particles expand, enabling them to hold two to three times their weight in water. Perlite is a mined silica-type rock, which is also heated to expand it to tiny white beads that do not decompose readily and that function to hold water and aerate planting mixtures.

Containers

Food containers can be recycled for growing seed. Cottage-cheese or margarine tubs are excellent. Save the tops for saucers. Aluminum foil cake and bread containers are ideal. Even half-gallon milk cartons can be sawed in half, lengthwise.

If you bought annuals or perennials from the garden center last year, perhaps you saved the trays. They are good for seed planting. The chief requirements are depth, at least 2 to 3 inches, and drainage holes. Since the food containers will not have them, poke several holes in the bottom or bottom sides with a heavy nail, screwdriver, or ice pick.

All of the foregoing types of seed-starting containers involve two steps: seeding in one container and transplanting to individual pots when the seedlings have their second pair of true leaves.

Many have learned the shortcut method, that is, planting the seeds in individual pots. Several seeds are planted per pot, just to be sure at least one germinates. If several come up, the weakest will be cut off with scissors and the strongest one left to grow. (Never pull the unwanteds out, as this will disturb the roots of the seedling that will remain to grow.)

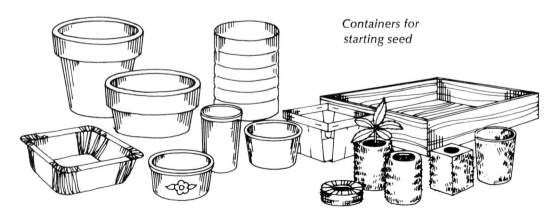

Containers for starting seed

This shortcut method works fine for inexpensive seed when there are quantities in a packet. But for rare or dustlike seed, the two-step method is best.

Individual pots are made of molded peat and vermiculite. They have to be filled with a sterile seed-planting mix first. The seedlings will remain in them "forever" because each pot is planted directly in the ground and will eventually decompose as the roots push through it. Another type of individual pot to plant directly is the peat wafer, which expands to a solid pot when soaked in a bucket of water. Seed is planted in it by scratching the surface to make a hole for the seed. Still other individual pots are the molded cubes of peat infused with plant nutrients. These are small squares and will need to be set into larger pots of soil as the seedlings grow. Otherwise, the seedlings become floppy and their roots do not develop well.

All individual pots must be arranged in waterproof trays—either aluminum cooking pans or molded plastic trays from garden suppliers. The pots are soggy and fragile and not meant for handling.

One prerequisite for planting is often overlooked: labels. Each seed flat or tray of individual pots needs a label. It's the only practical way to keep a record of what is planted. You should record the name of the seed planted and the date. Some people also like to note the seed source. Labels are available commercially or you can devise your own.

In Thomas Hyall's *The First Garden Book*, published in London in 1563, there is a gem of horticultural wisdom that many follow but rarely admit: "Sow seeds in the increase of the moon; cut down and harvest in the wane of the moon."

Whether moonstruck or not, before planting by either the one-step or two-step method, water the containers. Never sow seed in a dry planting mix. Place the seed trays in a pan of water or the kitchen sink and allow water to seep up to the top from the bottom drainage holes. They will be lightweight at first and may float, so you might have to weight them down. You can see the water come to the top. Remove from the pan and drain. Then you are ready to plant.

Seed that needs light to germinate is just sprinkled over the top. (Refer to the list on p. 56 to check.) Either tamp it gently out of the packet by making a V-trough with the packet lip or put all the seed in your hand and gently sprinkle it over the top.

If the seed is meant to be covered, then add just enough dry planting mix on top to cover it—no more than the size of the seed. Then water the seed pan again. Either resoak it (it won't take as long the second time) or, for fine seed, mist the top of the pan with a house-plant mister to soak the seed down in.

The next step is important for both methods, one-step or two. Slip each container of seed—either the cottage-cheese tub or the tray of peat pots—into a plastic bag, using one bag for each container. Seal it shut with the twisters provided and place where the seed is to germinate. The plastic bag keeps the planting mix evenly moist. You may not have to water again until the seed starts to germinate. The plastic bag also protects the seeds from drying air currents and the curiosity of small children and pets.

To germinate, the seedlings need to be in a warm place. Those that need light can be put right where they are to grow, even under fluorescent lamps. Those that are covered can

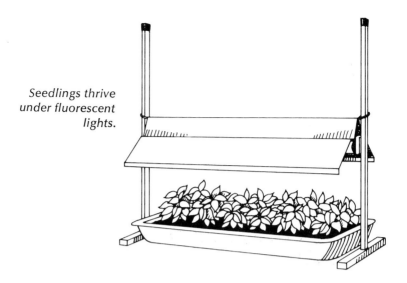

Seedlings thrive under fluorescent lights.

be put in an out-of-the-way place that is warm but where they can be checked frequently for germination. Walter Chandoha, the noted animal photographer, has great success starting his vegetable garden seed indoors by keeping his seed trays on top of the furnace until they germinate.

Once the seedlings germinate, the plastic bag is removed and the seedlings start the fascinating business of growing. At this time, it will also be important to keep them evenly moist but not soggy. A touch of the finger to the sowing mix is the best test. It should always feel damp, not wet. If the sowing mix has nutrients added, the seedlings should progress well the first few weeks.

If not, then start feeding once a week with a weak dilution of house-plant fertilizer at one-quarter the rate suggested on the label. Keep this up until the seedlings are ready to go outdoors.

Those following the two-step method will need to transplant seedlings to individual pots when they have their second pair of true leaves. A wooden or plastic label or top end of an old teaspoon makes a good seedling trowel. Frances M. Miner, former head of the instruction department at the Brooklyn Botanic Garden, always taught the youngsters to handle seedlings by a leaf. "Seedlings always have several leaves, but only one stem," she would tell them. It's a wise admonition for all gardeners, since seedling stems are very sensitive to injury by handling.

Seedlings grow fast. They will lean toward the light, so their growing trays must be turned around each morning to keep them straight. (Under fluorescent lamps there is no problem.) Tall, stalky plants such as snapdragon, seed dahlias, and even petunias will need to be pinched back to force them to branch. Wait until the seedlings are several inches high, then pinch out each terminal bud.

Toughening Time

When spring is in the air, there may be a rush to put the new seedlings outdoors. Never be hasty. Seedlings have been pampered indoors and have never known high winds, the full brunt of the sun, or chilling night air. Also, some seedlings are quite tender and can endure only the mildest conditions.

Some seedlings, such as calendula and pansy, thrive in cool spring weather and the sooner they are put out the better. Check the outdoor planting recommendations on seed packets and the references for each flower in the center of this book (see pp. 103–211).

But before any seedling is put outdoors— hardy or tender—it must be toughened up or hardened off, as the professionals call it. This is a gradual exposure to the big outdoors.

The simplest way to do this is to put the trays of seedlings outdoors for a few hours

Double petunia

each day, on the patio, back steps, or deck. Then take them indoors again. On a pleasant day leave them out all day. And finally, overnight, a day or so before planting.

Under Lights

All the foregoing also applies to starting plants under fluorescent lamps. The only difference is the source of light. Seedlings respond amazingly well to fluorescent light because the source is constant; there are no cloudy days, and the degree of illumination provides sufficient radiant energy to support growth.

There are all kinds of approaches to starting seeds under lights. If the lights are used primarily for a seedling nursery, then a makeshift setup can be arranged in a basement or workroom. Commercial home or industrial fixtures are fine. The best kind to use are the 4-foot reflectors which take two or three 40-watt tubes. Paint the insides white to reflect more light.

These can be suspended on chains and fastened with hooks so the level of the reflectors can be lowered and raised as the seedlings grow. The reflectors can be suspended above an old workbench, or even old cardtables for that matter. Be sure the fixture is plugged into a wall socket with a three-prong grounded cord for safety.

For a few seedlings, the commercial two-foot African violet growing stands are handy. Those who do not want to design their own light arrangements can buy ready-made units from mail-order catalogues or garden centers and discount stores.

Although there are numerous brand-name
horticultural lamps on the market, each with

assorted merits, seedlings will thrive with a combination of Cool White and Warm White fluorescent tubes available at almost any electrical supply store. The tubes come in 20-watt (2-foot) or 40-watt (4-foot) lengths to fit the fixtures.

The lamps should be left on at least 14 hours a day, or better, 16 hours. Cost estimates average $2 more a month on the electric bill. For convenience, the fixtures can be hooked up to an automatic timer that will turn the lights on and off at the designated hours.

When the seed is germinating, the lights can be very near the seed containers—as close as 2 inches. As the plants grow, the fixtures are raised so the lights are about 6 inches above the top of the tallest seedlings. The slower-growing, shorter seedlings can be raised on blocks of wood or overturned cottage cheese tubs to keep them close to the lights.

Be careful about watering seedlings under lights, as they tend to dry out more quickly because of the high rate of growth. Also, feeding regularly will be important, and experience will guide you on this.

4. soil preparation and planting techniques

Soil Preparation

Soil preparation tends to be taken for granted. Tyros may feel it is all rather unnecessary. After all, you dig a hole, put in the plant, and nature will take care of everything.

Actually, soil preparation is the most important part of gardening. It is the foundation, and results will be determined by how well things are started. Well-prepared soil allows abundant root growth and supplies the nourishment needed to keep plants thriving. When the soil is worked deeply, roots have an easier time pushing down. Plant growth is stronger. Deep roots have access to soil moisture, a vital point when there are droughts and local watering restrictions. Soil that is friable or easily crumbled is also "alive." It will support the bacteria, earthworms, and microrganisms necessary to break down organic components and to allow exchange of minerals in the soil's chemistry.

Garden soil has four essential components: water, air, mineral matter, and organic matter. How well these components are combined determines the quality of the soil. A fertile loam —the ideal—contains fifty percent water and air space. The other half is at least five percent organic material and the rest mineral matter. The minerals are from the parent rock that broke down eons ago in the process of weathering and aging.

The mineral matter breaks down into categories depending on the size of the particles. The largest—rock and sand particles—are easy to see and feel. Rub some soil between your fingers; those gritty rough portions are the rock and sand particles.

Wet the tips of your fingers and feel the soil again. If there is high clay and silt content, or a lot of organic matter, the soil will feel slimy and slippery. Soils with too much clay and not enough organic matter have a tendency to dry out quickly and pack hard in droughts. These small mineral particles—clay and silt—are difficult to see. So are the organic-matter particles. They tend to make the soil dark in color.

Clay and organic-matter particles are the workhorses of good garden loam. Organic matter is what makes a soil "granular," easier to dig and cultivate. It also increases the soil's ability to retain moisture. This is one reason why abundance of organic matter is essential for those who garden by the sea.

Clay particles are essential for their attractant ability. These tiny particles are charged and draw mineral nutrients to their surfaces and hold them for release when needed by the roots. A good balance of these two microscopic soil particles will make all the difference in the quality of plants grown.

The basic mineral character of any particular soil is impossible to change because it is dependent on the geology and rocks in the region. But the quality of any garden soil can be changed and this is what soil preparation is about.

Natural Soil Improvers

Few suburban or city gardens have enough organic content in their soil. One of the best soil improvers at hand is autumn foliage. If the soil can be prepared in the fall, there is no need to wait until spring, especially when a new flower garden is planned. Rake the fallen tree leaves on top of the soil and dig them in. A 5- to 6-inch layer of leaves is about right. The soil bacteria and microorganisms will go to work on the leaves immediately and start to break down before cold weather. Decomposition not completed in fall will continue in early spring long before you can get outdoors to work. If you have access to some stable manures, add them to the layer of leaves and turn it under, too.

Fall soil preparation is equivalent to the farmer's ritual of fall plowing, which allowed the land to lie fallow all winter to benefit from the freezing-thawing action which improves soil structure. If soil preparation must be delayed until spring, dig it at least three or four weeks before planting to allow time for the soil to settle. The time will also reveal how well the soil drains and whether there are any low spots to fill in.

If there is no compost or leafmold available in spring, peat moss is a good substitute. A 3- to 4-inch layer is adequate, but never apply it dry. Either spread it just before a rain so it absorbs moisture or cut an "I" slit in the bale and pour in a gallon or so of warm water. Let it stand overnight, and then spread it and dig it into the soil. Peat moss acts like a sponge if dug into the soil dry and will absorb the soil moisture rather than augment it.

If you can, also work in a several-inch layer of weathered manure (never fresh, as it could

Two-tone dianthus

67

burn sensitive plant roots). If aged manures cannot be located, the processed dried manures are good substitutes.

Drainage

Annuals and perennials grow best in well-drained soil. This means soil where water penetrates rapidly without standing puddles. Poorly drained soil is not well aerated, becomes compacted, and restricts good root growth.

These poor drainage areas are often in low spots or where the subsoil is compacted, with no aeration or "pore" spaces. A drainage layer of gravel, potsherds, or pebbles may help if placed 8 to 10 inches or so below a flowerbed, if you insist flowers must grow there. But generally, avoid planting flowers in these places. Selected shrubs that can tolerate wet roots are a better choice.

Fertilizer and pH

While digging in the organic materials which improve the soil, you should also consider fertilizer, which supplies nutrients for the plants. A well-balanced garden fertilizer such as 5–10–5, at the rate of 3 to 5 pounds per 100 square feet, is good. The high middle number, phosphorus, is important for good flower production. The first and last numbers represent nitrogen and potash.

Soils in the northeastern United States tend to be acid and usually need applications of lime every few years. If the soil has not been limed in recent years, it may be practical to spread 3 to 4 pounds of ground limestone per 100 square feet.

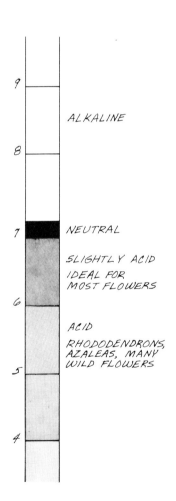

9

ALKALINE

8

7   NEUTRAL

SLIGHTLY ACID
IDEAL FOR
MOST FLOWERS

6

ACID

RHODODENDRONS,
AZALEAS, MANY
WILD FLOWERS

5

4

The pH rating is a scale that measures the acidity, neutrality, or alkalinity, with pH 7 being neutral. Numbers below are acid, those above are alkaline. Most flowers require a soil pH reading of 6 to 6.5. Plants that require a more acid soil, below 6, are woodland species that thrive in the deep loamy soils, while some plants such as blueberries, rhododendrons, and azaleas thrive in very acid soil (to pH 4.5).

Soils in the Southwest tend to be alkaline, while those in the Midwest are usually nearer neutral. If there is a doubt about the soil, there are simple soil-test kits available at garden centers for a nominal sum. Or full soil tests are usually available from the state agricultural colleges or from the local county offices of Cooperative Extension.

The major soil preparation as described is for the start of a new flowerbed, whether for annuals or perennials. If portions of a garden are going to be revamped, the same rules apply. The better the soil preparation, the better the results.

If a perennial flower border or annual bedding section is to be revitalized or changed in its color scheme or pattern, the pockets of soil where the old plants will be taken out and the new ones set in can be dug and prepared just as though it were a new bed. In time, the entire garden could be revamped. When dividing old clumps of perennials, never replant the divisions without renewing the soil first.

Planting

Times have changed. It once was that plants that bloom in spring were planted in fall and plants that bloom in fall, in spring. But the advent of container-grown nursery stock, including annuals and perennials, has changed much of this ritual. Now many plants can be moved from the time the soil can be worked until early fall—even while in full bloom.

It may seem an amusing idea to set out flowers willy-nilly. But, the garden will look willy-nilly by the middle of summer if you don't follow through and plan as shown in chapter 2. A flower garden deserves planning. When planting time comes, the diagram you have prepared can be used for setting out the plants in their proper spaces.

For a major installment of a new flower border, this is the only way. If the border is long and wide, work at it gradually. If plants are ordered from mail-order nurseries, set them out in their designated places as they arrive. Mark these areas carefully with labels. Then fill in with the other plants as they arrive.

If a shipment of plants arrives during inclement weather, remove the perennials from the carton. Check them over carefully. If the plants appear dry, trickle some water into the top of the wrapping but do not unwrap them. Set them in a cool, light place—sheltered indoors—until they can be planted. When the plants are set out, they should be watered in completely—muddied in, as the nurseries describe it. This means making a mud puddle around the plants to eliminate soil air pockets and assure good contact of soil around the roots.

Also be guided by the weather. Some plants are hardy and can be set out as soon as the ground can be worked. Others are tender and their planting must be postponed until the ground is warm and the nights are not too chilly. A flower garden does not have to be planted all at once. Just be sure to leave the proper spacing for the fill-in plants when their planting time comes. And always keep a record of what is planted where, even if you think you'll remember. Make use of the plastic label that usually comes with plants. Your planting diagram for the garden is the best place to make notations. When plants are set in place, underline or circle them as a notation. The plans will be good records to keep for future reference if the garden is ever changed or if there are errors or failures to replace.

Before setting out any plants, examine them carefully to see how they grow. If the new shoots and roots are closely joined, the plants grow from crowns—where roots and stems meet. Pansy, delphinium, daylily, and hosta are examples. These crowns or joints must be kept at soil level. If set too low or high, the plants will not survive. To accomplish this, always keep the crown at soil level with one hand while the other works the soil into the planting hole and around the roots. Firm gently and water them in.

Terminal shoots are the growing points for most annuals. They are at the top of elongated stems: zinnias, marigolds, and snapdragons are examples. The soil line is not critical when planting these seedlings.

Perennial roots are now retailed in dec-

Plants which grow from a crown, left, are set at soil level, while those that grow from a terminal shoot are set more deeply.

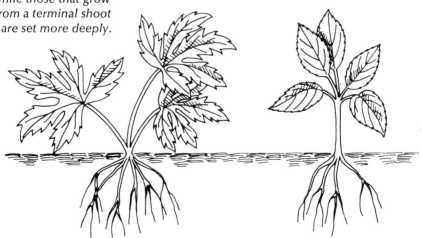

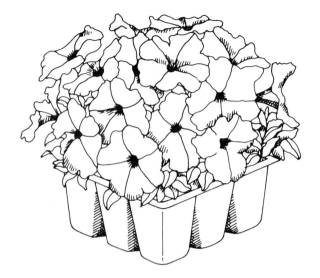

*A pack of petunias
in full bloom,
ready to plant*

orative boxes packed with sphagnum moss.
Sometimes they are completely dormant, or
shoots are starting to sprout by the time the
plants are sold. Examine the roots and tops
carefully. Pull away the packing to avoid breaking off the fragile tops. Any thin, broken, or
browned shoots should be cut off. Also, examine the roots to be sure they are firm and
intact. Break or cut off any mushy, weak ones.
Then set the plants in the prepared planting
hole, firming the soil around the roots carefully.

Annual seedlings sold in bloom have been
a tremendous boost for consumers, who can
see exactly what they are getting. Examine
these plants before purchase. Avoid weaklings
with spindly stems even if the flowers are
large. These seedlings, called transplants, are
sold in strips of peat pots, trays of small plastic
pots, individual four-inch pots, or six-packs.
Use an old kitchen knife to cut through the
soil of the six-pack containers to separate the
annuals to squares of soil.

If the seedlings are growing in individual
peat containers, there is no need to remove
the seedlings from the peat pots. They decompose in the soil and the plants' roots will grow

through them. But soak these peat containers in a bucket first before planting. Also work them a bit to make them more pliable. This hastens the breakdown in the soil, and roots break through them more easily. Never allow an exposed portion of the peat pot to remain above soil.

If you grow your own seedlings in the expandable discs that form individual peat pots, such as the Jiffy 7's, pull off the plastic netting from these peat pots before planting and also soak them in a bucket of water. The netting does not biodegrade and many a retarded annual has been pulled up at the end of a summer only to discover its peat pot still intact and the roots confined.

When annuals and perennials are planted, always water them promptly. Water settles the soil around the roots and provides the moisture necessary to get them off to a growing start.

Tools

Every gardener adds a few tools each year, no matter how hard he or she tries to stay away from that section of the hardware store or garden center. There is always a new gadget that appeals or a proper tool that does a special task.

The basic tools seem to remain constant and few gardeners can get along without them. They include a sturdy *spade or garden fork,* or both. Look for a spade with a turned step at the top of the blade. It's easy on the foot if there is a lot of digging necessary. The garden or digging fork also does a worthy job of digging and turning over soil. It is also handy for turning compost and breaking up heavy soil clods.

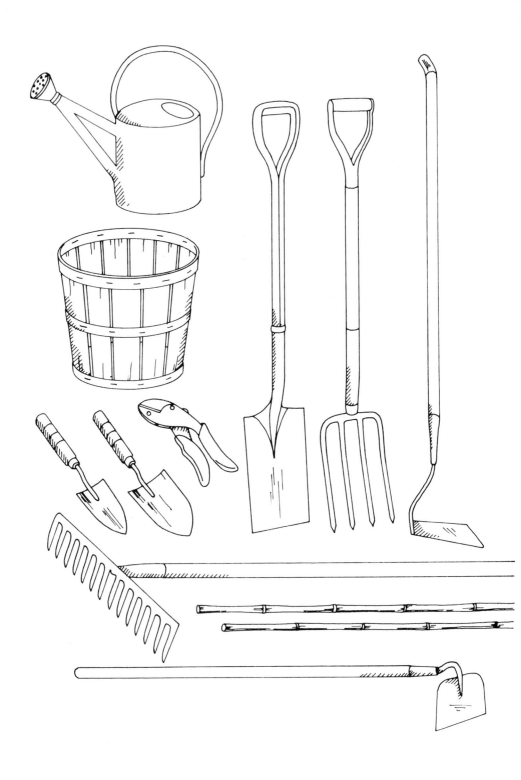

*Basic tools for
the well-equipped
gardener*

A sturdy *rake* is used for working the soil back and forth and smoothing it level for planting. Select a well-built steel rake with either a bow-head or flat-head. This heavy rake cannot be used for raking leaves off the lawn (for this a flexible-steel grass rake or bamboo rake does a good job).

It is handy to have two *trowels,* one with a wide blade for setting out large plants and seedlings and the other with a narrower, thin blade, which is useful for planting small seedlings and little bulbs. Be sure the trowel is of sturdy quality—stainless steel with a molded handle.

A long-length *hose with a lawn sprinkler* will save much time and effort when there are droughts. An oscillating sprinkler can be set up to provide a light rainfall over the flower border. Or invest in a soil-soaker, either the closed-end plastic type with perforations every few intervals or the old-fashioned canvas soil-soaker. The water wand is another hand-hose attachment to reach into wide flower beds. It has a control valve at the handle.

A good set of *shears* will be needed to cut down perennial stalks in fall, either lightweight pruning shears or heavy clippers.

You will need a large *basket or lightweight garden cart* for cleaning up trash and carrying it to the compost pile.

Although mulches go far in keeping down weeds, one extraordinary tool deserves special mention. This is the indomitable British invention called the *Swoe,* a combination scuffle hoe and hoe, which is masterful in cutting off weeds at soil level and cultivating the soil lightly. It will also chop weeds to a fine pulp. The Swoe has a long hollow steel handle and a stainless-steel blade that will last your lifetime and perhaps that of your grandchildren.

5. keeping up the garden

Once the planning and planting are done, the garden comes alive. Green shoots push up. Young seedlings put out new leaves. The first flowers open. The commitment is final. There is no turning back. Tending begins. And so does the pleasure of spending idle hours and even busy hours watching over your garden. Working around plants is a gentling process; it filters out the day's tensions. Even such a nuisance task as weeding tiny snippets of grass from flagstones provides satisfaction, a sense of accomplishment.

When you garden, you observe the earth closely; your work complements that of nature by helping with the hose when rainfall is scarce, adding nutrients to the soil when plants are ready to flower, taming growth when nature's exuberance takes over. Keen observation can often spot trouble before it becomes rampant. Many an insect population may be routed or a fungus disease prevented by being aware of what is taking place and solving it with quick action.

76

Spring Cleanup

Winter deposits debris on the garden—leaves, twigs, and tree fruits. Wait for a good bright day to tackle the uncovering of mulches and be sure to wear old shoes, or better, rubbers, for the ground will be mucky and damp no matter how fair the sky. Time this deed wisely. Wait until some of the spring shrub buds start to open or swell. Forsythia is a good indicator that spring is truly arriving and that most of the harsh freezing-thawing weather has passed. When this signal appears, the mulches can safely be removed from the perennials. Lift off the evergreen boughs, salt hay, or straw and add them to the compost pile. If the mulch is autumn leaves, pull it aside and assimilate it into the soil later on.

Removal of the mulch will reveal stirrings underneath. Skinny red-green shoots of bulbs and perennials will be poking up. There may be remains of last year's leaf stalks and old foliage. Pull or cut these off and discard them in a separate pile for the trash, not the compost pile, just on the chance that there may be some leftover insect eggs or fungus spores hanging on.

Fresh air and sun will dry off the new shoots and the soil around them. This is the time to cultivate the soil around the perennial crowns, but do it ever so lightly. Some perennials are shallow-rooted and the new shoots are tender. Also, some perennials, such as platycodon, are so tardy emerging in spring that you may trample them underfoot before they have a chance to appear.

Light cultivating with a long-poled or hand tool aerates the soil and opens it to allow moisture to penerate the roots more easily. If plants were heaved (pushed up) by alternate freezing and thawing of the soil, press them back lightly with your hand or foot. (Mulches should prevent this.)

While cultivating, apply a spring tonic of fertilizer to the perennials. Bulbs should not need it if the soil is in good condition. Apply fertilizer with some judgment. Quantity will depend on how well the ground was prepared when the plants were set out, their age, and how well they have grown. New plantings may not need additional fertilizer, while older, established gardens most likely will.

There are several choices. Some gardeners are satisfied to use only superphosphate in the spring if they know that their soil is fertile. Where soil is marginal, others may use a balanced fertilizer such as 5–10–5. Organic gardeners may prefer bonemeal, dried blood, and wood ashes. A few rely totally on animal manures.

If commercial fertilizers are used, follow the application rates suggested on the bag or box. Experienced gardeners can often judge how much fertilizer to apply to perennials in spring. They find that a band of complete fertilizer traced around the perimeter of the plants and worked lightly into the soil with a cultivator is sufficient.

Thinning

As spring warms up, the skinny new shoots will also green up. With some perennials, there will be too many, particularly the tall background plants such as asters, veronicas, phlox, and maybe peonies. They will need to be thinned out. To do this, reduce the number of shoots per clump to about a half dozen (more for peonies, however). Simply cut out the

Thin shoots of too-thick perennials by pinching them in spring at ground level.

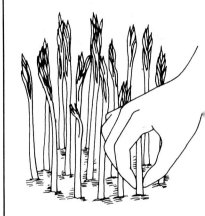

weaklings with a sharp knife or pinch them out between thumb and forefinger. This simple step will go a long way toward promoting strong uncluttered growth and better bloom. If the clumps are allowed to remain too thick, growth is spindly, the stalks are weak, and bloom is less than spectacular.

Pinching

This term describes a manual kind of plant pruning to encourage branching. Some annuals—zinnias, snapdragons, asters, impatiens—and some perennials—chrysanthemums and asters—must be "pinched." Otherwise they develop into a skinny stalk topped by few flowers.

Pinching is removing the terminal bud or growing point by pinching it between thumb and forefinger. This deed will stop plant growth at that point and force side shoots to develop at the nodes where the leaves are attached.

Most annuals, such as snapdragons and asters, need one pinching. Pinch them as seedlings when they are 3 or 4 inches tall. Perennial chrysanthemums and asters need at least two pinches, the first when the young plants are 6 or 8 inches tall. When these new shoots have grown 6 inches or so, then pinch out the growing point of each new shoot. This second pinch should be done by midsummer (early July) to allow the plants to develop bushy growth and set flower buds for fall bloom.

Disbudding

This is another form of manual pruning and does the opposite of pinching. By removing

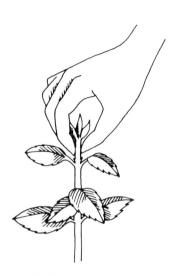

Pinch out terminal shoots to force branching.

the side buds from peonies, and allowing one single center bud to grow, you can force the strength of the plant to form one huge flower per stem. Pinch these buds when smaller than pea size.

The same is true of chrysanthemums. The "football" 'mums so popular at collegiate football games are induced this way. The greenhouse growers pinch off all side buds to force one flower bud per stem to grow. This practice is best left for 'mums grown in the shelter of a greenhouse.

Watering

The main point to keep in mind with watering is not to neglect it. When annual seedlings and young perennials are set out in the spring, they are watered in to settle the roots. This initial start, plus the usual spring rainfall, is generally sufficient to support young plants and established plants into the summer season.

When the rainfall tapers off, it's your turn to take over. Water is a valuable resource. When you get out the hose or watering can, be sure to make it worthwhile. A good, deep soaking once a week, without rainfall, is much wiser than little sprinklings when you think of it. Deep watering makes roots grow deeply for penetration to near subsoil levels where excess water supplies are stored.

The rate at which soils will absorb moisture varies and no predetermined schedule can be laid down for how long and when to water. Clay soils are poorly drained and water takes a long time to penetrate. Sandy loams are sieves and water rinses right through them. The best way to retain water in sandy soils is to add and keep adding organic matter— mulch, peat, compost, even seaweed.

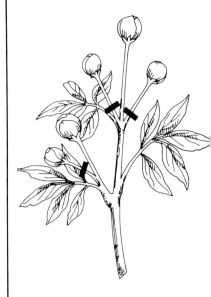

Remove the side buds of peonies when they are the size of peas to encourage larger flowers.

80

If the flower garden is large, a soil-soaker is an easy way to water, and the least wasteful. There are two kinds, either a plastic hose with holes punched along it or a long, thin canvas "sock." Both attach to the hose and trickle out water as slowly or as fast as the pressure allows. A soaker can be left in place until the soil is wet through to at least 4 inches, then move it along to the next place.

Lawn sprinklers do an excellent job of watering, too. Droplets simulate rain. The type that can be adjusted to "fit" the shape of the flower garden is best.

If the garden is only postage-stamp size, or just a few containers on an apartment balcony, then a good, large watering can will do.

There is no sense debating what time of day to water. It rains at night and if night watering is convenient, go ahead. If there is an extremely hot spell, however, then early morning or mid afternoon is best because the droplets will not evaporate in the heat of midday.

One final point: In gardens where there is poor air circulation or where mildew disease is often a problem, then ground watering, not overhead sprinkling, is preferable. Humidity and moisture on foliage encourage mildew, especially on zinnias and phlox.

Grooming

As the garden grows, good grooming is essential. Yellowed and browned leaves should be removed whenever they are seen. When flowers fade, snip them off. This is vital not only for appearance but to prevent the formation of seedpods. Seedpod formation is the signal to a flowering plant that the growing season is over and flowering stops. Petunias, snapdragons, pansies, and many other annuals are "eager" to form seedpods, even if it is only the middle of summer. When they do, that will be the end of their flowering season, unless, of course, you are diligent about pinching off old flowers. Don't just pull off petals, for the seedpod could develop. Pinch off the entire faded flower head.

There are exceptions. Recent bedding plant introductions, particularly begonias, certain marigolds, and impatiens, are what the seedsmen term "self-cleaning." They are pollen sterile and can never set seed. So their flowering continues until frost ends it.

Another reason why it is so important to remove faded flowers from all plants is because, as a general rule, seed development takes a great deal of strength from a plant. Seedpod formation also leads to unwanted seedlings. Seedpods ripen, spill their seed, and innumerable unwanted volunteers take hold. If left to grow, unwanted seedlings become a nuisance, overcrowding the desired plant, and, because they are selfed (fertilized by their own pollen), they are inferior to the selected parents of the original variety. Only in rare instances are the overpopulating selfed seedlings welcome.

Giant pansy

Midseason Feeding

There is a knack to knowing when plants need additional fertilizer. Too much fertilizer can be just as faulty as starvation. Flowers that look vital and appear strong and vigorous are undoubtedly growing in soil that was prepared properly before planting. They don't need any more help. Additional fertilizer should be considered a booster. It is never a substitute for poor soil preparation.

Some big feeders, such as peonies, delphiniums, and chrysanthemums, need a light application of fertilizer at midpoint during the growing season—the peonies and delphiniums after flowering and 'mums while growing and setting flower buds.

Flowers growing in containers—on terrace and patio tubs, on city penthouses and terraces, in hanging baskets, and in window boxes—also will need supplemental feeding. Their soil space is limited and the mass of roots that build up in this confined space rapidly absorb what soil nutrients there are. Container plants can either be fed once a month with a regular application of water-soluble fertilizer or, even better, can be kept on a constant feed schedule. This method supplies a very dilute rate of fertilizer once a week, with plain water in between.

Plants will indicate when there is need for supplemental feeding. Signs usually are pale or yellowing leaves, slow or weak growth, and fewer flowers. Experienced gardeners learn to recognize these signs and apply remedies. The quick-acting, water-soluble fertilizers are best for small gardens, and for immediate results. For extensive plantings where an overall effect is important, use remedial fertilizers such as superphosphate or sodium nitrate to correct phosphorus or nitrogen deficiencies, or a complete fertilizer such as 5-10-5 to boost sluggish growth. Two pounds per 100 square feet or 1 teaspoon per square foot works well. Water well after applying.

Staking

Plants should not appear to have crutches, but some of them are so rampant and lanky that they need help to look their best. Also, thunderstorms and wind can wreak havoc in an unprotected flower border. It is up to you to disguise plant supports as well as possible. The top of the stake should be several inches below the crown of the plant.

The easiest kind of staking to disguise is natural staking, that is, branches and twigs saved from pruning fruit trees, shrubs, and hedges. The ideal natural stakes come from privet. They always seem to grow straight up and branch at just the right places to support asters, daisies, coreopsis, rudbeckias, and other floppy perennials.

The tall, erect, and stately kinds, such as delphiniums, foxgloves, snapdragons, and dahlias, can best be supported by single bamboo stakes, which may be bought inexpensively at garden centers. A supply of them will last for years if they are pulled up and stored at the end of each season.

Peonies may or may not need staking. In some old-fashioned gardens where the plants are decades old, I have seen hedges of these magnificent plants unstaked, strong and upright. In more confined areas, where the peonies share the soil space with other perennials, they often need support just to keep them within their allotted space.

Conceal the stakes of delphiniums so they do not overshadow the bloom spikes.

Summer Mulches

The mulching task fulfilled will, more than any other, contribute to your tranquillity during the long summer when the beach, golf course, tennis courts, open roads, trails, and seas beckon. Those who mulch carefully can enjoy their recreation with a free mind. A mulch is nature's own caretaker. It is a covering over cultivated soil to keep roots cool and soil moisture in.

The greatest benefit of a mulch is that it smothers weed growth. Weed seeds are ever present in the soil, scattered there by winds and animals. If the germinating weed seed has only a thin layer of soil to reach the light and sun, it thrives until uprooted. But a weed seed does not have enough vitality to push up through soil and another two- to three-inch layer of mulch. The result: It doesn't make it and expires.

Mulching material for flowers needs to be chosen carefully. The functional type used in a vegetable plot has no aesthetic appeal. Whatever helps to bring in the harvest, fine. But the flower garden is a showplace and the mulch must be appropriate.

One natural mulching material that has great appeal is fine-grade bark chips or wood chips. These are widely available at garden centers. Some utilities sell them, especially in spring after they have pruned trees to clear winter-storm damage. Chip mulches should be about 2 inches thick, certainly no deeper than 3 inches. Apply them with this caution: The bacteria that break down the woody bark fibers consume vast quantities of nitrogen in the process. Supplemental nitrogen—either sodium nitrate or ammonium sulfate—is important to prevent chlorosis, or yellow leaves. Follow directions provided on the fertilizer bag and apply a month or so after mulching.

Another convenient mulching material, if locally available, is pine needles. They are attractive and functional. Partially decomposed compost is also excellent. The coarse-textured humus can be lightly spread over the planted area. Ground corncobs, chopped tobacco stems, or bagasse (sugar-cane pulp) can be

Star petunia

85

utilized as mulches in areas where they are easily obtained and inexpensive.

One mulch to avoid for flowers is black plastic. Unattractive and a nuisance to put down and take up, it is better suited to vegetable gardens. One exception might be municipal park systems, which find the black plastic mulch an excellent labor-saving device when planting large flowerbeds. The black plastic is spread over the ground after the soil is prepared. Annual seedlings are set into holes cut in the plastic and watered. The entire bed is covered with a layer an inch or so deep of bark chips to weight down the plastic and disguise it.

This method can be adapted for a home garden flowerbed of annuals if it appeals. The planting diagrams must be worked out first so the pockets for the plants can be cut in the plastic in the right places.

A better idea, the ultimate in summer mulching, is the chipped leaf system used by Frederick McGourty, Jr., editor of the Brooklyn Botanic Garden's handbooks. He is a weekend gardener who, by necessity, had to work out a practical maintenance method for his twelve-acre property in northwestern Connecticut. Three acres are intensely cultivated with perennials.

Fred invested in a leaf shredder, which is stored in his barn. When the autumn leaf litter settles down, the collection is raked up and put through the shredder, which chips the leaves into tiny pieces.

The mulch is piled to one side until spring. If the pile is soggy come spring, it is roughed up with a pitchfork to dry it off. When the flower planting is completed, and the beds have been checked over, the chipped leaf mulch is put into place—a 2- to 3-inch layer.

The mulch looks handsome, and it functions extremely well to keep moisture in and weeds out. Furthermore, Fred McGourty does not need to add extra fertilizer to his garden. Over the years he has observed a few instances when chlorosis developed in heavy-feeding perennials, but he corrected it with additional nitrogen. In his experience, the leaf mulch provides enough soil nutrients and organic matter to maintain a magnificent flower garden. This type of mulch breaks down in a season and must be replaced every spring. The only cash is the initial outlay for the leaf shredder, somewhere between $200 and $300, depending on size and horsepower.

Dividing

Dividing is a deed that tries a perennial flower gardener's patience. For a perennial is just that, a plant that lives for many years. As it lives, it grows. It develops underground stems, all of which have eyes that develop into new shoots. Thick mats with woody centers form; in time, the perennial loses its vitality and, if not divided, fails to flower. Most perennials need this attention. A few, bless them, do not. But we would all be foolish to restrict ourselves to such carefrees as bleeding heart, peony, platycodon, and flax.

As with shrubs, a good rule to follow on perennial dividing is "after they bloom." This would mean spring perennials are divided in early summer, plants such as iris and Oriental poppy in midsummer, and fall-blooming perennials the following spring. Some perennials, such as chrysanthemums, need division every spring. Others, such as heucheras, asters, phlox, helenium, Shasta daisies, astilbe, and physostegia, need division at least every three years.

If in doubt whether or not to divide plants, take a good look at them. If there appears to be a knotted mat of leaf stems and dead woody centers, and if bloom has been less than spectacular, the plant most likely needs division.

The ideal time to tackle the job is after a good rain, when the soil is moist and easy to dig. The entire root clump of the perennial has to come out of the ground to divide it properly. You can't do it "in place."

To get at it, dig around the entire root clump with a spade; thrust it straight down all around the perimeter to cut off any running side roots.

Once the roots are freed, get under the clump with the spade or a spading fork and push up. Wiggle it free and pull it out of the hole.

If the root clump is not too large, pull it apart with your hands, breaking it up into several substantial pieces for replanting. If the clump is too overgrown, you may need to wash off the soil with a hose to examine the roots more carefully.

Too-old clumps will have a hardened core of dead, dried stems and roots, with the vital viable portions around the edge. Cut off these strong young sections and discard the old center. Use either a sharp knife or pruning shears.

Before dividing, have a wet piece of burlap handy. Then cover the healthy root pieces with it to prevent them from drying out. Prepare the new planting spaces and set the healthy roots in place at the same soil line at which they were growing. Water well. This is an important follow-up immediately after planting to settle in the roots. Also check these plantings every few days to be sure the soil is sufficiently moist—but not soggy—to promote good establishment of the roots.

If you have more pieces of viable root divisions than you can use, avoid making the mistake of stuffing them back somewhere in the garden. Share them with a neighbor or a fellow gardener. You'll both be happier.

Stem Cuttings

In late summer, many annual plants can be induced to lead a double life by rooting stem cuttings to become winter house plants. Coleus, geraniums, impatiens, and begonias do well as pot plants. Cuttings taken a month before cold weather and frosts root more easily. Cut pieces of stem, preferably those that have not flowered, about 5 or 6 inches long.

All of them will root easily in water if the container is kept in bright north light. Or the cuttings can be inserted in premoistened perlite or vermiculite, or a half-and-half mixture

Use a sharp, clean knife to take cuttings from healthy shoots of a geranium plant.

of the two. Roots will form in two to three weeks. Then the new plants can be potted in a sterile potting mixture and grown indoors in a sunny place, or under lights.

This technique is also a good way of carrying over particularly appealing annual flowers for the garden next summer. As the plant grows larger during the winter months, several more cuttings can be rooted from it to provide numerous plants large enough to set out in the garden the following spring. A favorite geranium, or impatiens with an unusual flower color, can be kept practically "forever" this way. It's called cloning!

Replacement

Sometimes plants fail—both annuals and perennials. Either they are ravaged by insects or disease, or they are weathered out by too much sun, shade, rain, or drought. Their disappearance can make an ugly gap in a flower garden. When these voids occur, they can be filled in with mature seedlings from garden centers. Most nurseries now make a practice of carrying a limited supply of annual bedding plants for just this purpose. Most often they are potted individually and can be popped into spaces wherever they occur—in terrace tubs, borders, or window boxes—to keep the continuing show of flower colors. If you don't fill in the spaces, nature will—with weeds.

Hybrid geranium

Flowers to Dry

By hanging: Cut the flowers in midmorning when they are half open. Arrange the stems in small bunches so the heads are free and tie them together with soft twine. Large flowers are hung singly. Hang them upside down in a cool, dry place. If there are many flowers, the strings can be hung like laundry on a clothes-line, or several bundles of tied flowers can be fastened on coat hangers and hung from nails. The flowers will dry in a week or two, when they should be taken down and arranged. The bottom leaves are usually stripped from the plants when dry.

The following plants are particularly suited to drying by this method:

Astilbe	Marigold
Baby's breath	Spider flower
Blanket flower	(seedpods only)
Candytuft	Strawflowers
Cockscomb	Yarrow
Honesty	

By dehydration: Thick, many-petaled flowers dry best if they are placed in a desiccant, either a mixture of half Borax and half corn-meal or the commercial product silica gel (this is a form of ground quartz mixed with absorbents and is sold under several trade names). A layer of the material (either one) is placed in a large dress or suit box. The flowers, shorn of their long stems, are placed face up or face down, whichever allows them to lie flat. The drying material is carefully sprinkled over and around the petals until each flower is fully covered. Cover the box and do not disturb for four to six days. The flowers are dry when crisp to the touch. Remove them either by lifting each flower head carefully or by gently pouring the mixture out of the box. Use florist wire to put proper stems on the flowers for arranging.

The following plants are well-suited to drying by dehydration:

Aster	Delphinium
Bachelor buttons	Loosestrife
Balloon flower	Marigold
Calendula	Pinks
Canterbury bells	Shasta daisy
Chrysanthemum	Speedwell
Coneflower	Strawflower
Coral bells	Sunflower
Cosmos	Zinnia
Dahlia	

Fall Cleanup

When the flowering season wanes, a gradual tuck-in for winter begins. Essentially you will be doing chores in the fall that might be done in spring; but by doing them properly in autumn, you will bypass a lot of problems. Spent annuals are pulled up and composted. Yellowing and fading stalks of perennials are cut down to 3 or 4 inches. This stubble provides anchoring for winter mulches. Foliage of any plants that have had disease problems, such as mildew and botrytis, should not be composted but should be discarded with trash. Pull up, clean, and store all plant stakes, and if late-rising plants such as platycodon, are not clearly labeled, mark them with a label for spring reference.

Winter Protection

Timing is the key. Winter protection should be done late enough in the season to keep plant roots cold and the soil frozen. The object of winter protection is not to warm plants but to keep them cold, to maintain the status quo. If the soil freezes early, by Thanksgiving, the perennials can be mulched. In some areas, soil does not freeze until late December and the boughs of the Christmas tree are treasured for covering the perennial garden.

The winter mulch serves its greatest function in "false" springs when the ground thaws in winter and plants are stirred. The ground heaves at night, the temperature plummets back to winter, and exposed plants are often damaged or killed. A winter mulch covers the susceptible perennials and shields them from this damage.

Some plants have evergreen leaves or succulent crowns. If they are covered with too much mulch they are smothered and often suffer from winter rot. Canterbury bells, delphiniums, Oriental poppies, anchusa, and foxgloves are best protected with an airy mulch such as evergreen boughs and pine needles or salt hay tucked under the foliage to keep it well aerated. Never be too hasty in removing these winter mulches. Be sure spring has truly arrived.

Pests and Diseases

Just when everything seems to be doing well in new flowerbeds, strange things sometimes happen. Leaves show gray spots. One plant in a patch wilts while others stand tall. Leaves have holes made by unseen feeders.

These signals of pest or disease invasion are the troubles that frustrate and challenge. Disease-causing organisms may already exist in a new garden, remnants from previous cultivation, or they may be introduced with new plants. Weather can encourage their develop-

Aphid

ment—humidity, excess rainfall, drought, poor air circulation, and even air pollution.

Insects are mobile; they get around easily. Most of them are winged or at least good crawlers. Many travel as wind-borne eggs or nymphs (as gypsy moths do). Other insects winter over from one year to the next on weeds and debris that is transported to and fro. A few just crawl into the garden.

Good garden housekeeping is the best way to prevent disease and insect problems. The reminders outlined in the spring and the fall cleanup sections underscore this point. Gardens that are kept clean grow clean. Any diseased plants, such as asters or zinnias affected with mildew, asters ruined by yellows, or peony foliage marred by botrytis, should be hauled away to a town refuse collection point.

Be your own garden inspector when buying annual seedlings or perennials. Check the plants over thoroughly. Buy clean, healthy stock with full green leaves and good buds. A big plant is not always the best. Choose quality stock and order from reputable nurseries and mail-order sources.

Consider "sale" plants carefully. Often they are not bargains but stock that has been reduced for good reason. They may be diseased, poorly maintained at the retail source, or insect-infested. Occasionally end-of-season "close-outs" are legitimate sales, and nurseries cut prices on stock just to unload overhead.

Visit your flower garden frequently. Spend time enjoying it and "seeing" your plants, so you can develop early-warning antennae. Know how to spot troubles and identify their causes. Quick remedial action, a fast rescue effort, is often sufficient to stave off an epidemic.

Mealy Bug

Thrips

Slug

94

Whitefly

Mite

ORGANIC SPRAY RECIPE

Never be too hasty to take a major approach to a minor problem. One caterpillar on a geranium leaf is not a mandate to spray the entire garden. Kill the caterpillar on sight; it might be the only one around.

Insects will not frequent gardens where they are not welcome. Odorous sprays concocted from items on the kitchen shelf have been successful for vegetable gardeners to keep insects away and they will work just as well in the flower border.

Here is a recipe that was sent to George J. Ball Inc., seed and supply wholesalers, by Robert D. Rodgers, a tradesman who has had over fifty-five years of experience working with plants. His organic concoction keeps his plants insect-free in the greenhouse and outdoors. Here is his recipe:

Grind up in a blender 24 ounces of garlic and mix well with 16 tablespoons of mineral oil. Let stand 24 hours. Dissolve 2 ounces of Ivory soap shavings in 1 gallon of water. Add garlic-oil mixture and let it stand overnight. Mix well. Strain through a cloth. Add 1 part of this mixture to 10 parts of water in a sprayer and apply to plants weekly. If insects are already present, use every 3 days for control, and then weekly thereafter. Mix a fresh batch for each application.

CHEMICAL MEASURES

If you prefer a chemical approach, then it is imperative to know specifically what the insect or disease problem is and the precise pesticide recommended for its control. This

Japanese Beetle

95

attitude, careful study of the pesticide label, and proper follow-through in spray application earn high marks with any environmentalist. It is the indiscriminate and careless use of any pesticide that generates censure and causes needless problems.

Recommendations on disease and pest control can vary from county to county as well as from state to state. The media—both print and radio-TV—are doing an excellent job of providing local gardening "hot lines" when particular problems occur. They will often give recommendations for combating local insect and disease problems when they occur. These public-service features are often prepared and presented by professionally trained horticulturists.

Another excellent source of help is the County Cooperative Extension Office, which is usually located in the county seat. This nationwide network is connected to the United States Department of Agriculture and each state's agricultural university. It distributes the college's agricultural bulletins (which can also be obtained directly from the college). The staffs have access to the latest research, which in turn is passed on to individual homeowners. These offices also update state regulations and restrictions on pesticides.

A catalogue of garden bulletins published by the state university can be requested. They are either free or available at nominal cost to state residents. Addresses to write to are on page 255.

Pesticides are divided into categories that define what they control. The two that involve the flower gardener are insecticides and fungicides, and sometimes miticides. These chemicals are available either as wettable powders or as emulsions to be diluted and sprayed on

Tank sprayers are practical for easy application of liquid pest and disease controls.

plants. They are also manufactured as dusts for dry application to foliage. The pesticide labels will provide this information and clear directions for their use.

Here are some of the most common products considered safe for home use. Trade names are capitalized.

Insecticides: These work as stomach poison on chewing insects such as caterpillars and beetles or as contact poison on sucking insects such as aphids, leafhoppers, and thrips. Among them are Sevin (carbaryl); malathion; Spectracide (diazinon); resmethrin and tetramethrin (synergized pyrethrins); Orthene (acephate) and rotenone.

Fungicides: These chemicals halt the growth of fungi which cause molds, mildews, rots, and blights. Among them are captan; Fermate (ferbam); Phaltan (folpet); Karathane and zineb.

Miticides: Kelthane (dicofol) is used for severe infestation of mites.

The newest types of pesticides are the systemics. These chemicals are absorbed and then passed to other parts of the plant. They are either sprayed on the foliage or applied to the soil in granular form and watered in. They are effective for control of sucking insects such as aphids, leafhoppers, leaf miners, and mites. Many of them are toxic chemicals limited to professional use only. Two considered safe for home gardens are Cygon (dimethoate) and Metasystox-R (oxydemetonmethyl). Orthene (acephate) also has some systemic properties. The fungicide Benlate (benomyl) is a systemic for control of powdery mildew and other fungus diseases.

The new systemic pesticides can be scattered on the surface of the soil and watered in.

98

ON THE ALERT

Following are lists of some of the common diseases and insect pests that are encountered in a summer season, together with suggestions for controlling them.

Disease and Plants Affected	Description	Control

Botrytis
  peony
  geranium
	Grey mold on fading flowers and foliage; young shoots and buds blacken and rot	Cleanup of flower stalks in fall; remove mulches early in spring for aeration; spray peony shoots biweekly, 2 or 3 times in spring

Crown rots
  delphinium
  larkspur
	Several species; accentuated in hot muggy summer; plants blacken and rot at the crown	Remove diseased plants; practice good sanitation; no chemical control

Leaf spots
  cockscomb
  columbine
  chrysanthemum
	Spots appear on leaves, especially in rainy season	Zineb, after rain; remove diseased foliage

Powdery mildew
  aster
  phlox
  zinnia
	White coating on leaves; prevalent in damp humid summer	Benlate, as soon as it appears

Rust
  chrysanthemum
  hollyhock
  snapdragon
	Brown rust spots on undersides of leaves	Zineb, clean up and burn badly infected leaves

Yellow
  aster
  marigold
	Entire plant yellows and wilts	Plant resistant varieties; pull up and destroy infected plants; control leafhoppers which spread the yellow virus

Pest and Plants Affected	Description	Control
Aphids calendula nasturtium	Small insects called plant lice with sucking mouth parts	Malathion
Beetles marigold zinnia	Many forms of beetles invade gardens, particularly Japanese and Asiatic; they have chewing mouth parts	Control in lawns first, their breeding territory; hand pick or use malathion
Borer iris	Most serious pest of iris; eggs laid on foliage and hatch; larvae tunnel down to rhizomes which they hollow by their feeding; offensive odor is caused by a bacterial soft rot	Sanitation in fall and spring; spray young foliage twice in spring with Cygon or malathion at 2-week intervals
Borer, stalk dahlia zinnia	Hollows out thick flower stems such as zinnia and dahlia; undetected until plant flops over	Clean up weeds and foliage in fall to prevent overwintering eggs; slice open infected plants to reveal borers and destroy them
Leaf miner columbine	Tiny larvae of flies make white tunnels in leaves	Malathion or Meta Systox-R on young plants
Mealybug coleus impatiens	White-bodied insects with sucking mouth parts; cluster in leaf axils and on backs of leaves	Malathion at weekly intervals until controlled
Mite, red spider ageratum hollyhock impatiens phlox snapdragon	Minute spiders prevail in hot dry weather; leaves look dusty, yellowed, cobwebs on undersides	Kelthane

Pest and Plants Affected	Description	Control

Slugs
  hosta
  hollyhock
  seedlings
	Snails without shells prevalent in wet springs and summers; devour plants or eat enormous holes in foliage; work at night	Shallow saucers of beer or yeast trap and drown them; trap under boards, orange rinds, or banana peels and destroy

Thrips
  daylily
  iris
	Minute insects that suck leaf sap; cause streaking in foliage	Spectracide

White fly
  ageratum
  geranium
	Tiny white flies cluster in great numbers to feed on backs of leaves; take off in a cloud when plant is disturbed	Synthetic pyrethrin sprays (resmethrin); repeat every week to 10 days until controlled

the flowers

When it is considered that there are over 235,-000 species of flowering plants in the world, narrowing them down to a mere one hundred herein does seem to be presumptuous. However, the choices were made with good reason. These garden flowers have withstood the popularity test for years, possibly for a century. They are available from commercial sources. They can be grown easily to reward with colorful blooms and may even please with sweet fragrance. They will bolster the tyro's enthusiasm yet add to the experienced gardener's expertise.

Some flowers respond generously to small effort. Others require more attention. A few must be coddled. The turns, dips, and curves on the way to success with each have been pointed out in this section so the path to a beautiful flower garden should be easy to follow.

Many old-time favorites will be found here as well as some that may be new. Part of the pleasure of growing anything is that a venturesome spirit may meet the challenge of trying something different and succeed.

This selection of one hundred annuals and perennials has two obvious omissions: bulbs, both tender and hardy, and flowering shrubs. These types of plants require a book each; but they should not be overlooked in any garden plan, for they are an important part of the gardener's world.

the annuals

African daisy
(*Arctotis stoechadifolia*)
Sunflower Family

A dramatic 2-inch daisy from South Africa, it poses atop ridged, stiff stems about 18 inches tall. Forms a rosette of soft woolly leaves, some resembling those of calendula, some toothed, pale on back. Undersides of the petals are dark while the tops are cream, pink, apricot, red, or bronze. The centers have dark eyes and the flowers close at night. Definitely a sun lover, it blooms from late summer to frost. Good for sandy soils near the shore and excellent as a long-lived cut flower. Seed germinates in 3 to 4 weeks. Start indoors 8 weeks before warm weather and outdoor planting. Two months to bloom. The blue-eyed daisy (*Arctotis grandis*) has larger flowers and leaves and is a bit taller. Cut flowers often to keep them blooming.

Bachelor buttons
(*Centaurea cyanus*)
Sunflower Family

Perky fringed daisies stand on 2-foot wiry stems with thin ash-gray leaves. Best loved in its electric blue color, there are also pink, rose and white varieties. From the Mediterranean and Near East, it is the national flower of Germany and a close relative of dusty miller and wild knapweed. It has escaped from gardens and can also be found growing wild. English maidens wore bachelor buttons as a symbol of their eligibility and gentlemen favor the flowers as boutonnieres. The Latin binomial honors Centaur, the half-man, half-horse of Greek mythology who is said to have used the flower to heal a wound in his foot. An excellent cutting flower, it is easy to grow from seed planted directly where it is to grow. Hardy seed can be sown outdoors in fall to germinate in spring for early flowers. Sow again in spring for succession bloom. Grow in full sun. It does not transplant easily. The plants become sloppy and look best if faced down with a showy edger such as dwarf marigolds or sweet alyssum. Remove faded flowers often to prolong bloom, which lasts until hot, humid summer weather.

Begonia
(Begonia semperflorens)
Begonia Family

The old-fashioned wax begonia (always flowering) of grandmother's drawing room has become a high-fashion garden annual by the skillful work of hybridizers. The new types have vigor and stamina, and are glorious show-offs for shade or semi-sunny places. They are ideal for borders, pots, tubs, window boxes. Plants form high mounds of color with light green, dark green, or bronze foliage contrasted with flowers ranging from white to pink, red, rose, and combinations. Some have outer margins of contrasting color (picotee) or some are lined with white. A few varieties have double flowers. Blooms are weather resistant and self-cleaning, dropping the faded blooms naturally. Most hybrids are sterile, do not set seed, and flower continually until hard frost. Seed is extremely fine: 2,000,000 to an ounce and difficult to start indoors. Transplants from garden centers are more practical. Natives of Brazil, these begonias do best in well-drained, fertile soil enriched with compost or humus. Space dwarf (6–8 inch) plants 4 inches apart, in-betweens (8–10 inches) 6 inches apart, and tall ones (12 inches), 8 to 10 inches apart. Feed every 3 weeks. Take cuttings of side shoots that have not bloomed in late summer to root for house plants.

Browallia
(*Browallia americana*)
Nightshade Family

A perky annual from tropical America, it bears the name of John Browall, an eighteenth-century Swedish botanist and bishop who knew Linnaeus. The flower-growing bush type, 6 inches tall, has small flowers, less than an inch, in soft blue to almost purple shades. A good edging plant for semi-shade. Better known is sapphire flower (*B. speciosa*), 1 foot tall and spectacular when used for a hanging basket. All of these flowers have five petals which form a wide star. Colors are white or blue to purple shades with a white eye. Leaves are markedly veined and glossy, and taper to a point. Start from seed indoors. Do not cover the seed. Germination will occur in 2 weeks. Bloom in 2 months. Set outdoors when the weather is warm. Flowering continues to frost. Grows best in light shade on an eastern exposure and is somewhat tolerant of hot spells if watered and fed regularly. Pinch back to keep compact and blooming, especially as an indoor plant. In warmer climates, they may self-sow.

Butterfly flower

(*Schizanthus pinnatus*)
Nightshade Family

Another name, poor man's orchid describes these pretty inch-wide flowers. All the petals seem different. The lower one slightly lipped, the mid petal wide with a blotched splash of yellow, and the topmost a solid color. Flowers may be copper, red, lilac, rose, white, or yellow. The foliage is a lovely green, deeply cut, and almost fernlike. Seedsmen have selected strains scaled down to 14-inch plants which are covered with branched spikes of bloom. Though easy to start from seed planted outdoors, hot weather does them in. More ideally suited to areas where days are warm and sunny and nights cool. In the Northeast, they are worth a gamble with an early start indoors 8 weeks before outdoor planting weather. Do not cover the fine seed but keep it dark to hasten germination in 2 to 3 weeks. Flowers will appear in 3 months. Transplant to a semi-shady site, 8 inches apart, where soil is fertile and moist. In milder climates, plants can be set out in late summer for winter bloom. An excellent flower for a cool greenhouse or try it as an unusual house plant.

Calendula
(*Calendula officinalis*)
Sunflower Family

This is Shakespeare's marigold: "The marigold, that goes to bed wi' the sun, And with him rises weeping." Calendula is a pot herb of many uses. The petals are dried and used as vegetable dye, especially for broth, and as a substitute for saffron. Calendula comes from the Latin calendae and refers to the long flowering season in ideal climates. Definitely a cool-weather annual, the gorgeous flat-topped, fully double daisies grow in splendid golden colors of orange, yellow, lemon, and apricot. Native to Europe, the Pacific Beauty strain grows 2 feet tall with 3-inch flowers. Foliage is oblong and soft green. A dwarf form grows a foot tall. The secret to success in hot summer climates is early planting and light shade. Flowering ceases with hot, humid weather. In milder climates, seed or seedlings can be planted out in late summer for winter flowers. Start seed indoors so seedlings are sturdy enough to set out early with pansies. Seed germinates in a week. Grow in full sun and water well. Cut first blooms quickly and pinch back plants to encourage branching. Excellent for cutting or for growing in a cool greenhouse. Aphids may become a nuisance.

111

China aster
(*Callistephus chinensis*)
Sunflower Family

A magnificent daisy for display and cutting. A member of the huge aster tribe, of which there are up to five hundred species, the annual has a separate genus derived from two Greek words *kalistos* and *stephanos*, meaning very beautiful crown. It was introduced from China to France in 1731 by a Jesuit missionary. Colors vary from shades of red-rose to nearly blue tones of lilac, lavender, and purple. Flowers can be anywhere from tiny 1½-inch pompons to 5-inch Cregos. Grow from seed which germinates in 10 days. Or start indoors 6 weeks before the outdoor planting season. Tall 2- to 3-foot varieties are best in the cutting garden while 1-foot China asters are good for late summer color in borders or containers.

Hybridizers have created several flower types: cactus with stringy petals, curled shaggy doubles, singles with yellow centers, and tiny pompons. Grow in full sun and fertile soil, and water well in dry periods. Asters are susceptible to two problems: wilt disease, a soil-borne fungus, and yellows, a virus spread by leaf hoppers. To bypass these problems, select wilt-resistant varieties described in catalogues and rotate them to avoid planting asters in the same place each year. Use sprays to control leaf hoppers and reduce chance of virus spread. If an aster shows yellow leaves and is stunted, pull it up and discard; do not compost, to prevent further infection.

Cockscomb
(*Celosia cristata; plumosa*)
Amaranth Family

Novelty annual grown in two forms. The airy and interesting plume type, *plumosa*, has a feathery look. Dwarf varieties are a foot tall; others 3 feet. Colors of red, gold, and rose reflect their tropical home. Another type, *cristata*, is a curiosity, a velvet-textured conglomeration of petals that suggest a cockscomb, coral, or brain. Colors are red or yellow and the foliage is sloppy. *Plumosa* can be quite handsome in a mass planting in full sun or in a cutting border. Plumes also dry well for winter arrangements. Easily grown from seed planted directly into the ground. Germination in a week; blooms in 2 months, to continue all summer. Water well during hot weather and keep weeds away. The plants are heat-tolerant and popular with park departments for their low maintenance.

Coleus
(*Coleus x hybridus*)
Mint Family

Foliage, not flowers, are the hallmark of coleus, sometimes called painted leaves or painted nettle. Of mixed parentage, the modern hybrids include a species from Java that provides the tropical appearance. Harlequin patterns of chartreuse, yellow, orange, salmon, pink-rose and maroon trace through leaves with lacy, ruffled and fringed edges. Spectacular in mass plantings. Square stems and opposite leaves identify the plant's family—mint—and suggest an important cultural tip: frequent pinching back to prevent flowering. Excellent F_1 hybrids branch from the base in dwarf (8-inch) and taller (1½-foot) plants. Outstanding strains are Saber, Dragon, Rainbow, and Carefree. Hard to start from seed because it is so fine; do not cover. Germination will occur in 10 days. Six weeks to good-sized plants. Or, better, buy transplants in spring. Excellent for borders, window boxes, containers and even hanging baskets. Leaf colors are strongest in light shade as they bleach out in full sun. Thirsty plants, they are quick to wilt, and should be watered deeply in dry spells. Be on the alert for mealybugs and aphids. Root cuttings in water in late summer to grow for winter house plants.

114

Cosmos
(*Cosmos species*)
Sunflower Family

Light and airy qualities are the appeal of this sun-loving daisy from Mexico. Excellent for cutting, the foliage resembles dill, and flowers are borne on thin wiry stalks. Colors are orange, tangerine, red, white, and pink in single and multi-petaled forms. The Giant Sensations (*C. bipinnatus*) are 4 feet tall and flowers are up to 4 inches wide. They often need staking. More accommodating are the Klondyke types (*C. sulphureus*) which are shorter, 2½ feet, with smaller flowers, up to 2 inches, and the foliage is prettier. Easy to start from seed sown directly, but since they are late-flowering, a head start indoors helps. Seed germination is also slow, up to a month, but flowers appear in 2 months and continue until frost. Grow in full sun; sandy soil is best so they are excellent flowers for beach gardens. Be cautious not to over-fertilize as it promotes foliage and delays flowering. Pinch plants when about a foot tall to encourage branching. Close kin of dahlias, they are relatively pest free.

Creeping zinnia
(*Sanvitalia procumbens*)
Sunflower Family

A domesticated wildling of Mexico and Guatemala, this diminutive zinnia mimic is sure to please. Easy to grow from seed sown directly when the ground is warm, it needs only a place in the sun and the merest patch of ground. A groundcover, rarely over 6 inches high, it tucks in narrow spaces between walks and buildings, drapes over patio pots, and hangs from window boxes. Individual flowers are less than an inch wide—mini zinnias with golden yellow petals and dark centers. Thin seedlings to 6 inches apart, water only in dry spells and watch them flower from summer to frost.

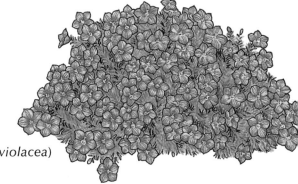

Cup flower
(*Nierembergia hippomanica violacea*)
Nightshade Family

Though perennial in Argentina, this charming tuck-in and edging plant is treated as a half-hardy annual. Flowers form a 6-inch spreading mound of inch-wide cup flowers that show off all summer and nearly hide the skinny leaves. An early start indoors 6 weeks before planting season will assure early flower display. Or buy transplants from garden centers. Germination occurs in 2 to 3 weeks and flowering in 2 months. Although full sun is ideal, some shade is tolerated; so are heat and drought. Try it as an edger, in rock gardens, in patio tubs, and in window boxes. Sensational as a hanging basket.

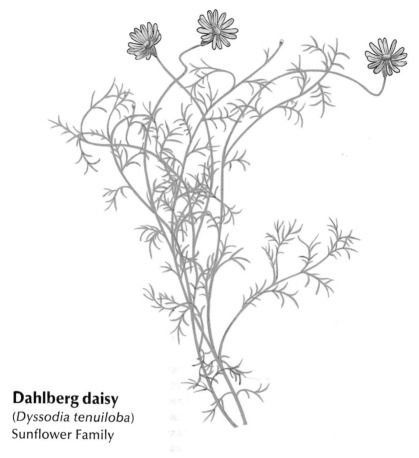

Dahlberg daisy
(*Dyssodia tenuiloba*)
Sunflower Family

Dainty describes this beguiling but difficult-to-find daisy that deserves much more garden space. The tiny half-inch flowers, also called golden fleece, poke out from low mounds of fine, lacy foliage. A charming edging plant that endures light shade, it grows less than a foot tall, but taller in full sun. A wildling in the Southwest and Mexico, it grows easily from seed but needs a head start indoors as it blooms late. Garden centers often offer started plants in spring. Best for all-season color in sandy soil where summers are hot. Rots out in too much moisture and cool weather. When pinched, foliage has a distinct odor.

117

Dahlia
(*Dahlia pinnata*)
Sunflower Family

The dahlia path leads two ways. Serious hobbyists can go all-out and plant tubers to achieve the giant plants with the dinner-plate-size flowers, a highly specialized procedure. Or, more fun are the dahlias that can be grown from seed. Called dwarf bedding dahlias, they are about 2 feet tall. The grow-from-seed hybrid flowers have rounded or grooved petals. Cultivars include the Coltness single hybrids on 18-inch plants; Unwin Hybrids, double and semi-double on 2½-foot plants; Redskin, a red 3-inch flowered variety with bronze foliage, 15 inches tall; and 3-foot tall Pompons. Colors are white, yellow, orange, pink, scarlet, and maroon, but not blue. Dwarf bedding dahlias need full sun and well-drained fertile soil. Seed germinates in 7 to 10 days and can be sown directly outdoors when the soil is warm. Or start it indoors 6 weeks ahead for earlier bloom. Flowering lasts from midsummer to frost. Seed-grown dahlias will form tubers by the end of the summer. These can be dug after frost has blackened the tops, dried, and stored to plant next year. Label them and keep the colors separate.

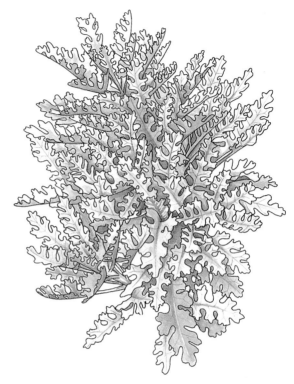

Dusty miller

(*Senecio species*)
Sunflower Family

Many plants are called dusty miller; the differences are in the shapes of
the leaves and the height and color of the tiny daisy flowers. All are
excellent relief plants grown for their gray foliage which artfully tones
down flower colors or accents them. *Senecio vira-vira* from Argentina
has leaves resembling those of the dandelion, rounded at the ends.
It is just under a foot tall and flowers are white. *S. cineraria* has more
deeply lobed leaves, is more silvery in tone, and its flowers are yellow.
It's about the same height and is a wildling from the Mediterranean
region. A third, Silver Lace, is a species of chrysanthemum and several
inches taller. The showiest of all, it has lacy foliage and is a fine textured,
delicate import from Grand Canary Island. Dusty miller is quite adaptable
to sun or shade and trouble-free. Buying plants from garden centers is
recommended to obtain a good supply and to have a chance to pick and
choose foliage textures. Seed is available but tricky to start. It needs
warmth, is not covered when planted, and is slow to germinate (2 to 3
weeks) and slow to grow. Plants are set outdoors when the soil is warm.
Space them about 8 inches apart.

Flossflower

(Ageratum Houstonianum)
Composite Family

Well named, these soft-tufted flowers sit in flat clusters above the stems. There are two sizes: dwarf, 6 inches tall; or a bigger plant 12-inch. Colors are marvelous purple-blue, sky blue, or white, and the leaves are heart-shaped and pretty. A wildling from Mexico and Central America, it thrives in sun or shade. In dry, hot spells water deeply to prevent wilting. The name is derived from the Greek *geras*, for old age, suggesting that the flowers continue a long time. They do, until hard frost. Good for cutting and superb for color in the border, as an edging, in window boxes, or in patio pots. If the center cluster browns, remove it to prolong constant flowering. Seed should be started indoors a month before outdoor planting weather. It germinates in a week if you do not cover it. Transplant outdoors when the soil is warm. Space dwarf varieties 6 inches apart; taller, one foot apart. It self-sows readily and can become a weedy nuisance in late summer. Flossflower is susceptible to white fly.

Flowering tobacco
(*Nicotiana alata*)
Nightshade Family

Spikes of this perky annual from Brazil will provide sweet jasmine scent, so they should not be wasted in distant borders. Put them near the house, by the patio, or in containers. Long broad leaves, hairy and somewhat sticky, are miniature replicas of tobacco (not for consumer use). The genus was named for Jacques Nicot, the French ambassador to Portugal who introduced tobacco to France in 1560. The foliage forms a cluster near the ground from which airy flower spikes grow. Each bloom is an elongated trumpet with a 2-inch star-shaped flare. Seedsmen have bred them to discipline their size and bad habits of flowering only at night. Two excellent strains are available: the Sensations, nearly 3 feet tall with colors of rose, lavender, mahogany, crimson, yellow, and white, and the appealing Nicki Hybrids, only 18 inches tall in rose, white, and pink. They are sensitive to frost, so do not plant seed outside until the soil is warm; otherwise, start seeds indoors 6 weeks ahead. Seeds are minute; do not cover as they need light to germinate in 2 to 3 weeks. Flowering begins in 6 weeks and continues to frost. Plant in sun or light shade. Space the larger varieties 18 inches apart and the shorter a foot apart. An excellent cutting flower, it will fill a room with sweet scent.

Four o'clock
(*Mirabilis Jalapa*)
Four O'clock Family

Also known as Marvel of Peru, this little-used annual from the tropics has
the curious habit of opening its flowers late in the day or earlier on cloudy
days. Related to bougainvillea, it has long tubed flowers of five fused
petals spread an inch wide, in delightful colors—mostly red, yellow,
or white tones sometimes with striped or flexed markings. The plant has a
bushy habit and grows about 2½ feet tall and as wide so give it room,
with at least a 12-inch space between plants. It grows in full sun, is
tolerant of dry climates, and is said to have some resistance to air
pollution. Sow seed directly where it is to grow when the soil is warm.
Germination occurs in 2 to 3 weeks. Flowering is from midsummer to
frost. The plant will form tuberous roots which can be dug and saved
for the following year to provide faster floral displays. In milder climates,
the plant will survive winters.

Gazania
(Gazania ringens)
Sunflower Family

These spectacular daisies from South Africa deserve to be better known. For open, sunny locations, they may be 3 to 5 inches wide and grow in bright colors of orange, scarlet, gold, pink, and red with brown centers. Each flower stands on a stiff stem up to 12 inches tall. The long leaves form a rosette at the base, dark green on top and soft woolly white underneath. The flowers close up at dusk and on cloudy days. When cut, the stems exude a milky substance. Named for Theodore of Gaza, a fifteenth-century scholar who translated Greek botanical writings into Latin, the flower is superb for large containers, window boxes, city terraces, and garden borders. Start the seed early indoors, 8 weeks before spring planting weather. A heat-loving annual, for bloom until frost avoid climates where nights are cool. Garden centers are starting to offer this dandy daisy and it is well worth hunting for.

Geranium
(Pelargonium hortorum hybrids)
Geranium Family

Since the introduction in 1963 of the first true from-seed geranium, Nittany Lion, named for the Penn State mascot, the common garden varieties (*pelargonium*) have made huge strides. Near the top of the popularity poll, they provide generous display all summer. A parade of F_1 hybrids continue to appear starting with the Carefrees, the Sooners, and the Sprinters. Natives of South Africa, these well-bred hybrids now have earlier flowers, weather tolerance, more vigor, and truer colors. Flower heads are huge, growing to five inches, and stand tall, well above the handsome mound of foliage. Flower colors are bright reds, rose, clear pink, salmon, and white. Gardens centers have enormous selections of transplants in spring. Or, for novelty, seed packets are sold for starting your own plants in January. Keep the seed warm—75 degrees—for germination in 2 to 3 weeks. They will respond rapidly under fluorescent lamps. Transplant to individual pots, and set outdoors when soil is warm. Geraniums prefer full sun although they will tolerate some shade. Feed once a month in borders or biweekly if in containers. The reward will be constant bloom until hard frost. Cuttings taken in early September will root easily for winter house plants. Use geraniums generously in containers, window boxes, patio tubs, and pots, in borders and in city gardens. Groom plants frequently, removing faded flowers and browned leaves to prevent fungus diseases from developing.

Heliotrope
(*Heliotropium arborescens*)
Borage Family

Just for nostalgia, this old-fashioned flower deserves space. Though a perennial, originally from Peru, it is grown as a summer border flower for its memorable fragrance. Andre Le Notre, the French landscape designer, made lavish use of it in the gardens of Louis XIV. The name refers to the myth that the flowers bend from east to west following the sun (*helio*) in a common plant response identified as phototropism, response to light. Some catalogues list it as cherry pie. The flowers are deep purple, fragrant, and clustered to suggest broccoli in bloom. The hairy, oval leaves are wrinkled. Plants can grow to 3 feet, although dwarfed selections can sometimes be found. Difficult to start from seed, heliotrope is usually available as rooted cuttings from quality garden centers specializing in unusual plants. Select a sunny place where the soil is fertile and cool. Hot dry climates are out. In early fall, take cuttings from the most fragrant plants and carry them over in a cool, sunny room or ideally, in a cool greenhouse. Plant outdoors again in spring when the weather settles.
(*Valerian officinalis*, a perennial with similar fragrance is also called heliotrope. It grows to 3 feet tall, has pink, white, or red flowers and fernlike foliage.)

125

126

Impatiens
(*Impatiens Wallerana*)
Balsam Family

Rare is the gardener who does not know this reliable solution for color in shade, even deep shade under maple trees. Also known as Busy Lizzy and Patient Lucy, the annual embraces several species from Tanzania and Mozambique with distinguishing characteristics: watery stems; flat open-faced flowers with five, somewhat heart-shaped petals; and a long tail-like spur on the lower sepal. Colors are marvelous: pink, rose, scarlet, coral, orchid, purple, and white, with some bicolors. Blooms are 1 to 2 inches wide and leaves somewhat lance shaped, soft textured, and lightly toothed. Watch for new hybrids from the tropical species brought back from New Guinea and Java; the leaves are extra long—to 6 inches—and the flowers huge by comparison—up to 3 inches wide. These new strains are also exceptions to standard culture and should be grown in full sun and fed frequently. In fall, impatiens plants form capsule seed pods which children love to pop and which results in yet another name for the plant, Touch-me-not. Hybridists have been busy. Scaled-down hybrids to 8 inches tall include Elfin and Futura series. For taller 2-foot plants look for the East African Holstii strains and the New Guinea types. Garden centers have ample selections of transplants in spring, but do not set them out until the soil and air are warm as impatiens are sensitive to the lightest frost. Or, seed can be started indoors 6 to 8 weeks ahead. Do not cover as it needs light and warmth to germinate in 2 to 3 weeks. Keep warm and moist. Impatiens need little care except during dry seasons; water them deeply and feed once or twice a summer. Take cuttings in fall to root for indoor house plants. Use as bedding plants, edgers, window box or tub plants, or in hanging planters. Another type, Balsam, has camellia-like flowers on 2-foot stems. Often used as a bedding plant in the South and in park displays, the foliage often smothers the flowers. The plants are also susceptible to wet rainy summers, and fade out.

Lobelia
(*Lobelia Erinus*)
Lobelia Family

A stalwart ground-covering annual that is smothered with one of nature's truest sapphire blue flowers. There are also varieties with sky blue, medium blue, rose, and white petals. Flowering never stops from late spring until frost. Leaves are grass green. Rarely over 6 inches tall, this carpeting delight from South Africa has curious tiny tubed flowers—three petals attached butterfly or "fairy wing" fashion to two minute rabbit ears. This lobelia is a close cousin of the wildling cardinal flower which grows in damp woodlands, an important clue to success: cool soil and semi-shade. Where summers are cool, lobelia can thrive in full sun. An excellent edging plant, it goes well with begonias and drapes beautifully from window boxes or hanging planters. Tricky to start from the fine, peppery seed, it needs 2 to 3 weeks to germinate. Start in late January or early February and do not cover the seed. More practical, buy started plants from garden centers to set out in cool spring weather. Space plants 8 inches apart, for continuous flowering until frost.

Love in a mist

(*Nigella damascena*)
Buttercup Family

This gentle flower from North Africa is much neglected. Its lovely mauve-blue flowers, 1½ inches wide, rest on a nest of cosmoslike foliage. Finely toothed petals lay one on top of the other, daisy fashion, and the center is a tuft of silky stamens. Even the 1½-foot-tall stems are trimmed with the feathery foliage, providing a mood of elegant grace. If you can plant this one early, as soon as the ground can be worked, all to the good, so that flowering gets a head start before hot summer weather. Provide full sun and fertile soil. Water well in dry periods. Sometimes called fennel flower, the black seeds will germinate in a week to 10 days and flowering should occur 2 months later. Blossoms appear for about a month. Space plants about a foot apart. Although mauve-blue is the prettiest color, there are also rose and white available. In the fall, the fascinating seed pods can be added to dried arrangements.

Marigold

(*Tagetes species*)
Sunflower Family

A wild flower of the Southwest and Mexico, their many kinds, colors, and sizes fill the pages of seed catalogues. The professionals' breeding tools are two species, the tall 3-foot African marigold (*T. erecta*) and the dwarf 1-foot French marigold (*T. patula*). Flowers come in many forms: single, fully double, carnation, chrysanthemum, and crested. Colors range from palest yellow to deepest orange and mahogany and combinations of these. Particularly fascinating are the triploids, crosses between the French and African types, which are 8 inches to a foot tall. They are sterile, horticultural mules, that never go to seed but flower until frost. The ferny marigold foliage has a dense odor caused by glands on the backs of the leaves. The variety Hawaii is odorless, however. Marigolds grow quickly from seed planted directly in warm soil where they are to grow. Full sun is best but they will tolerate some shade. Germination within a week. Thin dwarf-size seedlings to stand 4 inches apart, tall kinds a foot apart. Only the tall varieties need be started indoors and only to rush growth for their late flowering season. Chemicals from the roots will control soil nematodes. Use these annuals lavishly in bold borders, as edgers, as hedges, in pots, tubs, and window boxes.

Mexican sunflower
(*Tithonia rotundifolia*)
Sunflower Family

Named for Tithonus who was loved by Aurora, the goddess of dawn, this
huge annual from Mexico and Central America makes an excellent screening hedge or temporary divider plant. Four feet tall and almost as wide,
each plant is covered with large triangular-shaped leaves with velvety
texture. Late in the summer, the orange-scarlet single 3-inch daisies start
to form and shroud the plant with a gorgeous display. Easy to start from
seed, the variety Torch has good growing habits. Sow in an open sunny
place with average soil; the plant is both heat and drought tolerant. Since
the flowering is so late in the season, those in colder climates may want
to give the plants a 4- to 6-week head start indoors to speed flowering.
Germination is in a week to 10 days. Space the plants 3 feet apart to allow
room for their spread.

Mignonette
(*Reseda odorata*)
Mignonette Family

Fragrance, not spectacular flowers, is the specialty of this annual. Tiny ivory-white flowers shaded yellow, similar to those of sedums, form a cone-shaped cluster at the top of thick stems. Plants are about a foot to 18-inches tall and the leaves suggest those of calendula. Once grown extensively by the perfume trade for its fragrant oils, this tender annual from North Africa deserves to be tucked in among shielding plants that will hide its plainness. Use it in sunny places near doorways, in patio pots or window boxes, or in borders along a path. Easy to grow from seed, wait until the ground is warm and sow where it is to grow as seedlings will not transplant easily. Germination is in 2 to 3 weeks and flowers in 2 months. Thin seedlings 8 to 10 inches apart. Do not grow where summers are hot and dry as the seedlings will fade out before flowering. It does well in a cool greenhouse.

Moss rose
(*Portulaca grandiflora*)
Purslane Family

The fact that purslane, the ubiquitous garden weed, is a close cousin to moss rose emphasizes how easy this delightful plant is to grow. Give it a place in full sun, sandy or ordinary soil and a good soaking if summers are extremely dry, and the reward will be constant bloom until frost. A Brazilian import, it has all the sunny colors: orange, scarlet, yellow, rose, mauve, coral, and white. The short leaves are cylindrical and form a spreading mat, 6 inches high, over the ground. They are sprinkled with masses of roselike flowers. Some varieties have single rows of petals and the flowers of the newer hybrids are huge, to 2½ inches wide. Packets are usually sold either with mixed colors—the prettiest—or single colors. To grow this one, wait until the soil is warm. Select a broad open place such as a walkway, narrow border, or edging along the patio or a rough rock outcropping. Sow the fine seed thinly on top of prepared soil and press it in; do not cover. It will germinate in a week and flowering will begin in 8 weeks. That's all there is to it. The flowers will close in the afternoon—about teatime. And, if it's cloudy, they never do wake up.

133

Nasturtium
(*Tropaeolum majus*)
Nasturtium Family

These delightfully colorful flowers hail from the cool Andes. They have a sweet odor and bright colors: scarlet, orange, yellow, mahogany, and cream. In profile, the topmost petal has a long spur which appeals to hummingbirds seeking nectar. Leaves are mini waterlily pads. Purists can get mixed up in nomenclature with this one. Nasturtium is the generic name for watercress, a point worth keeping in mind considering the flower's leaves are excellent for salads and the flowers and flower buds, which contain mustard oil, are also edible. The buds can be pickled and used as a caper substitute. Linnaeus named the flowers for tropaion, suggesting that the plant had all the markings of a heroic trophy—shield-like leaves and golden helmet flowers. Children like to grow nasturtiums. The seeds are large and, like beans, must have warm soil for outdoor planting. Soak the seed overnight in water to speed germination which takes 10 days. Select a place in full sun where the soil is poor. Too fertile soil encourages foliage at the expense of flowers. Blooms should appear 6 weeks after germination and continue all summer. There are several types: Jewel, about a foot high with semi-double flowers; Gleam, trailing plants, excellent to drape over patio pots and window boxes; and Whirlybird, the newest, with flowers held well above the foliage. Aphids can be a problem, especially under the foliage.

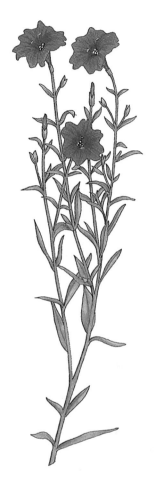

Painted tongue
(*Salpiglossis sinuata*)
Nightshade Family

If these dramatic flowers suggest petunias, you are on the right track, for the two are cousins. From Chile, it has lovely trumpet flowers with velvet texture. Colors range from buff, yellow, or orange to red, lavender, and purple with golden or cream penciling on the petals. The flowers are good for cutting. The stems are wiry, about 2 feet tall, and the leaves are sticky to touch. The flowers deserve much more use. Seed is fine, as with petunias, and should have an 8-week start indoors before the outdoor planting season. Do not cover but press it into the planting medium, keep warm. Germination in 2 to 3 weeks. Transplant as soon as the ground can be worked. Space seedlings about 8 inches apart. The sooner the plants get started in cool growing weather, the better. Cool moist nights and sunny bright days are ideal for best bloom. Relatively pest free.

Pansy
(*Viola x Wittrockiana*)
Violet Family

Happy faces of pansies—for thoughts—have appealed for centuries. Gerard notes that in France they are called "pensees." But it was not until the early nineteenth century that the fancy kinds appeared. Credit for the initial development goes to T. Thompson, gardener for Lord Gambier. Botanically, pansies are hybrids of three species of *Viola:* tricolor, lutea, and altaica. The hybrid bears the name of Professor Veir B. Wittrock, a Swedish botanist who sorted them out in 1896. Swiss, French, and Japanese breeders developed the beautifully marked hybrids grown today. The flower is never less than 2 inches wide and more often 3 or 4. Five petals form a flat, open bloom; the topmost are usually solid with the 3 lower ones a contrasting color or blotched to provide the pleasing "faces." Colors range from orange, gold, and yellow, to all shades of blue, maroon, red, and scarlet. Leaves are scalloped and pretty. Look for Swiss Roggli Giants, Majestic, Mammoth, and Paramount Hybrids. Favoring cool weather, pansies are best grown as biennials. In northern climates, seed is usually sown in July or August, wintered over in a coldframe or, in less severe climates, mulched with straw or evergreen boughs. In warmer climates sow in September for winter bloom. Refrigerate seed overnight and after planting cover, as seed must be kept dark to germinate in 10 days to 2 weeks. Plant outdoors early when large enough to handle. Pansies grow from crowns, like strawberry plants, so be careful not to "choke" them at the crown. Morning sun is best, never high noon heat, for longest bloom. Trim back so plants do not become floppy and remove faded flowers almost daily to prolong flowering into midsummer. Feed every 2 to 3 weeks and never allow plants to dry out. Pansies are good companions for early spring bulb flowers. Excellent for city gardens as they tolerate air pollution. Aphids and spider mites are sometimes a problem.

Periwinkle
(*Catharanthus roseus*)
Dogbane Family

Formerly classified as Vinca, this showpiece is challenging impatiens for popularity as a plant for light shade. A durable city flower, it withstands air pollution and needs summer heat. A tropical evergreen from Madagascar and India, its 1½-inch-wide flowers suggest huge phlox. Some are white with a red eye, pink with rose eye, or solid colors or white. The shiny foliage is handsome and deeply veined. The bush-type grows to about 1½ feet tall, but more appealing is the low-spreading, ground-hugging dwarf form, about a foot tall. A slow-growing plant, slow to flower, transplants from garden centers are recommended. To grow from seed indoors, you must start in February and keep pots in darkness for three weeks until germination. Take care not to overwater seedlings. An excellent groundcover plant for sunny areas as well as those in light shade. It also looks well draping from window boxes and patio pots and in hanging baskets. Feed lightly in summer. Trouble and pest free.

Petunia
(*Petunia x hybrida*)
Nightshade Family

The number one bedding plant, the petunia is a solid performer with rave reviews. The flower has come a long way from the ordinary rose-mauve flowers of grandmother's day. The modern hybrids sparked the imagination of plant breeders and led the way to carefully controlled inbred lines known as F_1 hybrids. There are two classes of petunias: multifloras, excellent bedding plants covered with 2-inch blossoms which have some weather resistance; and grandifloras with larger flowers—up to 4 inches—and often ruffled petals. Both classes come in single and double forms. The petunias are composites of several South American species with funnelform flowers—a trumpet of five fused petals. They have a mild fragrance and somewhat oblong smooth-edged leaves which are sticky. The plants form mounds about a foot high and come in colors ranging from deep purple, lavender, and lilac to all the shades of red, plus yellow and white. Many are striped or bicolored. The lists of varieties fill many pages of catalogues but buying transplants from garden centers in spring is much more practical. Petunia seed is minute, very slow starting and slow growing. Since indoor space is at a premium, save it for harder to find annuals. Petunias thrive in full sun, but tolerate some shade. Space them about a foot apart and use them everywhere: in beds, in borders, along walkways, in window boxes, in patio tubs and in hanging planters. Feed several times a summer to encourage growth. Groom frequently to remove faded flowers and prune back plants that become leggy. Aphids and slugs can be a problem, and in humid regions, botrytis, a fungus disease. Petunias sometimes self-sow, but rogue these plants as they will be disappointing.

Phlox
(*Phlox Drummondii*)
Phlox Family

Although there are about sixty species of phlox, many of them are superb perennials for the flower garden. One diminutive annual deserves mention. A wild flower of south central Texas, where it is called Texas Pride, it is a replica in miniature of the stately border phlox. In 1835, Thomas Drummond, an English botanist, was so delighted with the Texas flower, he sent seeds back home and the flower now bears his name. A dwarf plant which grows to 8 inches tall, it is ideal for edging, window boxes, and rock gardens. It does best in full sun and ordinary garden soil. Where summers are hot and humid, the plants sometimes fade out. Otherwise, they bloom until frost. Seed can be sown directly where it is to grow at a time when it is safe to plant lettuce. Germination in a week to 10 days. Thin to 6-inch spacing. Seedlings are difficult to transplant. Colors are lavender, rose, red, pink, and white. Some varieties have contrasting eyes or are bicolored. Particularly appealing is Twinkle with star-shaped flowers and serrated petals. To prolong bloom, pinch back faded flowers, feed lightly several times a summer, and water deeply in dry spells.

139

Pincushion flower

(*Scabiosa atropurpurea*)
Teasel Family

These perky, dome-shaped flowers on wiry stems have good colors: red, rose-pink, lavender, blue, and white. Prominent stamens poke out of the dense clusters of frilled petals to suggest a pincushion. The leaves are deeply etched and deep green. During the Middle Ages various species were used medicinally, especially to cure scabies. Native to the Mediterranean region and easily naturalized where the climate is ideal, this one is easy to grow and excellent for cutting. Provide a place in the sun and sow directly where it is to grow outdoors after frost. Seed germinates in 2 weeks and flowers appear in 3 months, to continue until frost. Or, seed can be started indoors a month before planting season. The Imperial Giants grow to 2½ feet tall and should be spaced a foot apart, while dwarf forms, 18-inches tall, are spaced 8 inches apart. Remove faded flowers promptly or cut them often to prolong the flowering season.

140

Pinks
(Dianthus chinensis. v. Heddewigii)
Pink Family

The delightful pinks, though mostly clove-scented perennials, include a
species from China that will bloom from seed the first year. The biennial
sweet william (*D. barbatus*) also belongs to the clan. Flowers are either
single or double with fringed edges which give the flower its name, rather
than the color. Bloom colors are red, pink, rose, or white, some with
contrasting centers. Low-growing with rubbery-textured, gray, grasslike
foliage, the pinks grow best in cool climates, especially where nights are
cool with ample moisture, although longer-flowering F_1 hybrids are on
the horizon. Foot-high plants are good for edgings or tuck-ins among
rocks. Pinks are easy to grow from seed which can be started indoors
early so seedlings have a jump on cool growing weather; germination is
in 10 days. Or, sow seed directly outdoors in fall for a head start on spring.
Grow in full sun; the sandier the soil, the better. They are good for
cutting; groom faded flowers frequently to keep plants blooming. The
dwarf varieties—8 inches—often look stunted unless the growing climate
is ideal. The foot-tall varieties are more appealing.

Poppy
(*Papaver species*)
Poppy Family

Two delightful poppies can be grown from seed. The Iceland poppy
(*P. nudicaule*), a wildling of the Arctic and alpine zones of this country
and Shirley poppy (*P. rhoeas*), a strain of the European Flanders Field
poppy named for Shirley Vicarage in Croydon, England. Both species
grow about 1½ feet tall and the flowers are 2 inches or so wide. Flower
colors are "electric": cream, rose, salmon, apricot, and scarlet, with silky
almost translucent petals. The gray-green foliage has rubbery texture,
looks rather feathery, and exudes a milky sap when cut. Packets of Shirley
poppy seed are available with single or double flowers while most of the
Iceland poppies are single and fragrant. Seedlings are difficult to transplant and the trick for success where summers are hot is planting them
early in fall. Seed of both species is hardy. It will winter over and sprout
in spring. Flowering will begin before the onslaught of hot summer
weather. Spring planting is fine where summers are cool enough for
flowers to withstand mid-summer temperatures. These poppies have a
bad habit of drooping their flower buds, but they will stand erect when
the petals open. To use them as cut flowers, cut the stems just as the
buds are about to open and seal the ends with a lighted match or dip
them in boiling water.

142

Salvia
(*Salvia species*)
Mint Family

The square stems of these popular border flowers are the give-away clue to their family membership—the mints. So are the large lower lips on the tubular flowers and mintlike leaves. Both annuals thrive in dry sunny soils with little care. For this reason, scarlet sage (*S. splendens*) particularly has endeared itself to municipal park systems and home gardeners to the point of cliché. An import from Brazil, the scarlet flowers are so dominant they overpower others in the garden and must be neutralized with companions such as gray dusty miller, sweet alyssum, and blue ageratum. More pleasing is the blue salvia (*S. farinacea*) with tall, skinny spikes suggesting lavender. This one is native to the Southwest where it is a perennial. Both salvias are widely available at garden centers for spring planting and should not be set out until the soil is warm. Flowering will continue until frost. Seed can be started indoors 6 to 8 weeks ahead of time. Do not cover it. Germination will take place in 12 days. Scarlet sage is available in sizes anywhere from a foot to 18 inches to 2 feet tall. Blue salvia is somewhat taller, to 2½ feet. Space small-sized plants 8 inches apart and larger plants a foot apart. Caution on feeding scarlet sage as it is subject to root burn. Scarlet sage will not "cut" for bouquets but blue salvia is handsome and can be dried for winter bouquets.

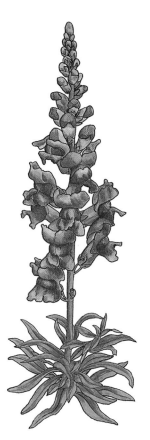

Snapdragon
(Antirrhinum majus)
Figwort Family

These curious flowers with an upper and lower lip add stately spikes to a summer display. Natives of the Mediterranean region, they have been so improved and selected over the past several decades, that almost any plant shape or color is available. They range in size from the dwarfs just 6 inches tall; to intermediates, especially the 2-foot tetraploids; to the handsome Rockets, 3 feet tall and more. The flower colors are superb velvet yellow, cream, gold, rose, red, scarlet, pink, lavender, or white, but not blue. The tall stems are lined with buds, the lower flowers opening first, then those above, until almost the entire spike is in bloom. They have a gentle fragrance, too. The leaves are somewhat oval and a lovely green. The newer hybrids also have inbred rust resistance to a disease that can be destructive. Garden centers have wide selections of transplants in spring, but if a special variety pleases, seed can be started indoors 3 months before planting season. Freeze the fine seed overnight. Thaw and plant. Germination in 2 weeks. Grow the seedlings at cool temperatures for a good start and set them out even when the weather is still cool. Full sun is best but they will tolerate some shade. Pinch back plants to induce branching. Feed once or twice a summer and if spikes start to form seed pods, prune the plants back and they should rebloom in a month.

144

Spider flower
(*Cleome Hasslerana*)
Caper Family

Brazil and Argentina are the home of this fascinating annual which deserves more use. An extremely showy plant it needs room in full sun and is spectacular planted in large beds. The name is derived either from its long, 2½-inch stamens, or the curious seed pods that form underneath the flowers as the old ones fade and new ones push up on the flower spike. The foliage is made up of five small leaves, but be cautious in handling their stems as there are pairs of short spines where they attach to the main stem. There are two varieties to consider. Rose Queen, with pink flowers fading to white, or all-white Helen Campbell. Give the plants space to spread. They reach nearly 4 feet and are about as wide. Sow the seed where it is to grow when the soil is warm. It will be up in a week and flowering will start in 2 months. Truly trouble-free and easy to grow, its display lasts all summer long. Self-sows and can become a nuisance if not watched over.

Stock
(*Matthiola incana*)
Mustard Family

What could be lovelier than spires of clove-scented flowers all summer? The secret to success is to beat the heat. A favorite crop for the florist industry, this import from southern Europe commemorates the name of Piersandrea Mattioli, a sixteenth-century botanist. It has been suggested that the name stock comes from the flower petals' resemblance to the stiff stock collars once worn by men. The flower clusters form in double petal rows on strong stems. Soft-textured, gray leaves are lance shaped. Ten-week stock, about 1 foot tall, will flower in 10 weeks from seed. Colors are blue, lilac, pink, purple, rose, yellow, and white. Somewhat shorter and quicker is Trysomic 7-week stock, which has some heat resistance, with similar colors. Where summers are hot, start the seed indoors 6 weeks before planting time. Germination will occur in 2 weeks. Set outdoors in full sun when the soil is workable. Space plants 8 inches apart. Seedlings with dark green, smaller leaves are usually single flowered and should be discarded to assure the most doubles. Where summers are cool, sow the seed directly outdoors and, in mild climates, treat as biennials. Sow in late summer for winter–early spring bloom. They are tops as cutting flowers.

Strawflower
(*Helichrysum bracteatum*)
Sunflower Family

A perennial from Australia, grown here as an annual, it has particular
appeal for flower arrangers. The straw-textured daisies dry extremely well
and can be used all through the winter months for colorful bouquets.
Bright flower colors: orange, red, gold, and bronze to deep purple. The
flowers average 2½ inches wide and the strong stems are about 3 feet tall
with deeply toothed foliage. A dwarf strain grows about a foot high. Give
these flowers good growing space in full sun, preferably a cutting bed.
Sow the seed directly where it is to grow. Germination takes place in a
week to 10 days. Thin, tall kinds grow to 18 inches and the shorter to 6
inches. Flowers will start to form in 3 months. To dry them, cut the blooms
just as the buds are starting to open. They will expand fully as they dry.
Strip the leaves and tie to hangers in small bunches to dry upside down
in a cool, airy place.

147

Sunflower
(*Helianthus annuus*)
Sunflower Family

An "annual flower of the sun," it occurs naturally in our western prairie states. A 10-foot-tall plant, the foot-wide flower and foot-long leaves have no place to grow but behind a garage or barn or at least along the back fence where there is some protection from high winds. There are smaller, scaled-down garden border varieties. Sow the seed directly where it is to grow when the soil is warm. Germination in 2 to 3 weeks. Space seedlings at least 3 feet apart. Water them generously and fertilize once a month to push them along. Flowering will begin in late summer. Mammoth is the most popular variety with heavy heads and good seed crop. To dry the flower head, cut it when the tiny florets start to wither. The outer seeds ripen first and the center core will still be green. Leave enough stem to attach a cord and hang the heads upside down in a cool place indoors to dry. They will shrink as they cure. Rub the flowers together to remove seeds and store them in a jar or closed tin.

148

Swan River daisy
(*Brachycome iberidifolia*)
Sunflower Family

A sweet-scented daisy from Australia that suggests a cineraria with dill foliage. Not widely grown, it is a delightful novelty to consider for sunny borders. Flowers are about 1 inch wide and seed packets have mixed colors: blue, lilac, rose, and white. Plants are a foot tall and should be spaced 8 inches apart so the stems can lend each other support. (Or use low brush for stakes.) Easy to start from seed. Sow directly in full sun where the daisies are to grow but wait until the soil is warm. Germination takes place in 10 days. Flowering will start in about 2 months and last for 6 to 8 weeks; it is a good plant for cutting to use in summer bouquets.

Sweet alyssum
(*Lobularia maritima*)
Mustard Family

A beguiling spreading carpet of white blossoms with a delightful fragrance
that blooms continuously until hard frost. Ideal for edging borders or as
an under-planting for geraniums, it may also be used to tumble over the
sides of containers and window boxes. A violet-colored variety is also
available. Alyssum is rooted in the Greek *alyssos* meaning "curing canine
madness." One of its virtues cited by Elizabethan herbalist, John Gerard,
is "It is given unto such as are enraged by the biting of a mad dogge
which thereby are perfectly cured." An import from the Mediterranean
region, it grows easily from seed. Germination occurs in 7 days, flowers
in 6 weeks. Sow directly outdoors as soon as the ground can be worked
in sun or light shade. It is a pest-free plant and generous, with little effort.
If plants go to seed and stop flowering, brush off or snip off the seed pods
and the plants will come back to full bloom.

150

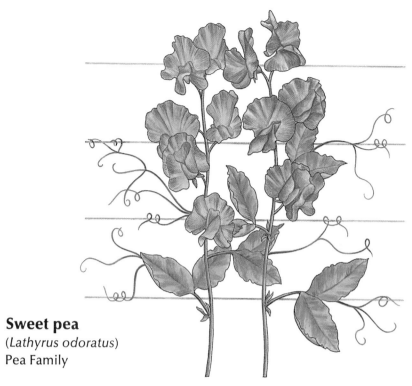

Sweet pea
(*Lathyrus odoratus*)
Pea Family

Hybridizers have been at work on the sweet pea for over one hundred years. There now are two major types: tall twining climbers that cling to supports by snaky tendrils, and the bush types without tendrils that do not need staking. The later are either Knee Hi to 20 inches, or the shorter Bijou and Little Sweethearts, a foot tall. Flower colors range from soft pinks to rose, scarlet, or purple to white—but never yellow. Each bloom—up to 2 inches wide—has a high Elizabethan-collar back petal, two wing petals, and the slip or keel petal typical of pea flowers. Four to 6 or 7 flowers attach to the stiff wiry stems which have no foliage. They need deep, rich soil, well-mulched roots, and cool growing weather. If the planting space is dug in fall and enriched with manures, it will be ready for digging and planting at the first spring thaw. Or get the jump on the weather and start seed indoors 6 weeks ahead. Germination takes 2 weeks. Space plants 6 inches apart, bush types 8 inches apart. Set a climbing trellis in place first to avoid disturbing the roots. Feed every 3 weeks with a high phosphorus-potash fertilizer (legumes such as peas make their own nitrogen). In mild climates, sweet peas are planted in late summer for fall-winter bloom. Pick flowers almost daily to prevent seed pods and prolong the season to midsummer. Aphids can be a problem.

Tahoka daisy
(*Machaeranthera tanacetifolia*)
Sunflower Family

Here is an instance when a common name is welcome for the Latin
binomial of this one is enough to discourage the most experienced
gardener. For a change of pace, and especially for flower arrangements,
try this big gorgeous blue daisy. A domesticated wildling from the hills
of the Dakotas south to Tahoka, Texas, which gave it its name, it
performs reliably for little effort. Flowers are about 2½ inches wide with
yellow centers. The foliage is similar to the common field daisy. About 2
feet tall, it grows easily from seed sown where it is to grow. A sunny site
and clay soil are ideal. Since the seed is hardy, it can also be planted in
early fall, for a good start in spring. Late flowering, it joins the tall marigolds and early asters which make good border companions.

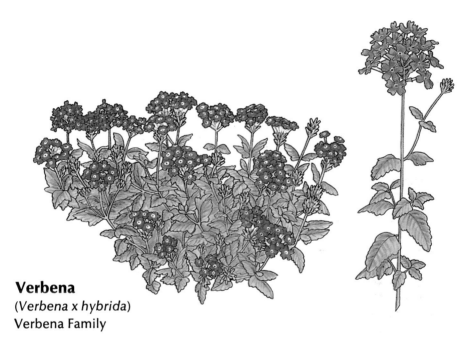

Verbena
(*Verbena x hybrida*)
Verbena Family

Dazzling is the word for this mat of color. The lightly fragrant flowers are available in shades of brilliant blue, scarlet, rose, pink, or mauve with white eyes. Each 2-inch blossom is a compact head of tiny five-petaled florets held on stiff stems, about 10 inches high. Handsome oblong leaves with toothed edges are a perfect background. A groundcover of the highest order for summer show, it has mixed parentage of several South American species. Plants spread to 18 inches and thrive in full sun, especially where the soil is sandy and gritty. They do well at the seashore. Transplants from garden centers are practical since seed is tricky to germinate, taking 3 to 4 weeks. Seedlings need coddling to get started. Set plants outdoors when the soil is warm and space a foot apart. Use lavishly to edge walks, trim patios, drape over window boxes and terrace pots, and face down mixed flower borders. Cut them often to prevent seed formation and maintain bloom all summer until frost.

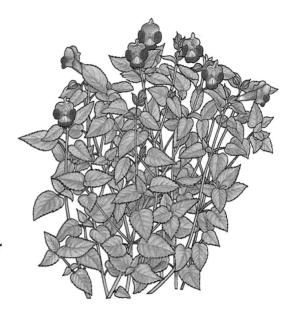

Wishbone flower
(*Torenia Fournieri*)
Figwort Family

Try this delightful plant from Vietnam for color in shade. Its other name, bluewings, hints of its charm. The tubular flowers have open-faced petals. The top-most is white to pale blue while the three basal petals are velvety-textured, deep purple with a yellow throat. Split the flower apart gently and you will see the two silky white stamens arched to resemble a wishbone. The foliage is lightly toothed and handsome. An ideal border plant about a foot tall, it was named for Reverend Olaf Toren, an eighteenth-century chaplain to the Swedish East India Company. Seed is extremely fine and slow starting; do not cover it when planting. Start it indoors at warm temperatures. Germination will take place in 3 weeks. Set out when the weather is warm or buy transplants from garden centers. Plant in cool, moist-shady or semi-shady places and space seedlings 8 inches apart. Flowering continues until frost.

Zinnia
(*Zinnia elegans*)
Sunflower Family

Gardeners who think they have brown thumbs should try zinnias. Even the seeds are large and easy to plant. This gloriously showy, happy flower is one of the most popular summer annuals. It bears the name of Johann Zinn, an eighteenth-century German botanist who was the first man to grow the seed in Europe. The original Mexican wild flower was a meager single daisy with washed-out lavender color. Hybridizers have done wonders with it. There are scores of varieties and sizes. Colors are sunny: orange, gold, yellow, scarlet, rose, cream, and white, with some bicolors or stripes, but no blues. Zinnias are as short as 6 inches or as tall as 4 feet. Flowers range in size from less than an inch to 5 inches wide. All have rough-textured foliage and flat flowers standing on stiff stems. Some hybrids resemble dahlias, some are cactus flowered with tubular shaggy petals. There are doubles, singles, small pompons, and buttons. Think warm weather and sun for zinnias. Seed outdoors directly where they are to grow when the soil is thoroughly warm since they are cold-sensitive. Germination in 5 days. Thin dwarf kinds to 4-inch spacing, medium to a foot spacing, and the tall giants to 14 inches apart. Pinch back young plants to induce branching. Flowering will begin in 6 to 8 weeks and continue to frost. Mildew which coats leaves with gray is sometimes a problem in hot, humid weather. Some tips on growing: Cut flowers often to keep them branching and blooming, water deeply if summers are dry, and feed several times a summer.

155

the perennials

Alkanet
(*Anchusa azurea*)
Borage Family

Those who are familiar with the wild flower viper's bugloss (*Echium*) may find a similarity as did Gerard with this flower of the Mediterranean region. He noted that, "The cups of the floures are of a sky colour tending to purple, not unlike floures of Echium." He also mentions, "Gentle-women of France do paint their faces with these roots." The Latin is based on the Greek, ankousa, to color or paint and the thick-fleshed roots do exude a red dye if they are cut or bruised. The flower is a glorious blue color, not unlike forget-me-nots. A tall plant, to 3 feet or more, with large coarse hairy leaves, and hairy flower stems, it tends to be less popular than other spire flowers. Search for cultivars such as Loddon Royalist. Plant in spring or fall where the soil is fertile and well prepared, and where it drains well. Full sun is best. Allow at least 2 feet spacing between plants. Divide every 3 years as it self-sows readily. Be meticulous about cutting off faded flowers to prevent volunteers and to encourage more bloom. Provide winter protection with salt hay or evergreen boughs as it tends to freeze out in severe cold winters.

Aster

(Aster species)
Sunflower Family

It is hard to imagine a perennial garden without asters. Undemanding and versatile, they suit almost any landscape need. Flowers range in size from less than an inch to 3 inches. Plants grow from 6 inches to 4 feet tall. Also called Michaelmas daisies, there are up to five hundred species to be found in the North Temperate zone, in Africa and South America. All have the characteristic daisy flowers that suggest a star—golden discs and ray flowers in blue-violet-lavender-rose-pink and white. The foliage is most often gray-green, lance shaped, and arranged alternatively on the stem. Grow asters in loamy soil enriched with rotted manures and compost. Full sun is best but they will tolerate light shade. Flowering starts in mid to late summer. Plant in spring and allow at least a foot between plants for small varieties, 2 feet for tall ones. Water well in summer droughts since asters should never be in dry soil. Mildew can be a problem in humid summers. Roots tend to mat and plants should be divided at least every 3 years. Discard the old center and split apart the younger greener shoots for replanting. Since the tall plants tend to be lank, pinch them back, as with 'mums, to keep plants in shape and full of bloom. Make the first pinch when new growth is about 10 inches high, and two more pinches each time 8 inches of growth is made. Also, too-thick shoots of spring growth can be thinned at ground level, leaving 6 to 8 per clump.

Astilbe
(*Astilbe species*)
Saxifrage Family

Everything is plus for this plant. Superb for shade. The compound foliage is handsome through most of the year. When the spires of blooms appear, the plants are a delight. There are so many cultivars, hybrids, and selections derived from a number of Asian species, that you can pick the plant color and size to suit the site. Choices range from 8 inches to 30 inches tall. Some of the finest hybrids were developed in France by Victor Lemoine and in Germany by George Arends both of whom worked with Chinese and Japanese species. The blooms are masses of tiny flowers formed into feathery plumes. Colors are lilac, rose, cream, pink, crimson red, and white. In fall, the foliage joins the oaks and maples and turns a bronzy yellow. An essential is deep moist loam soil enriched with well-rotted manures, compost, and peat moss. If summers are the least bit dry, water deeply, as astilbes must have moist ground. When flowers fade, cut the stalks to the ground to discourage self-sown volunteers. Divide the plants every 3 years, the best way to rejuvenate lackluster plantings. Feed every spring. Use them in clumps of 3 or 5 in a border or for a dramatic show mass them under trees or along drives. The blooms can be cut and dried if picked when half-open. Plant in spring or fall and space plants according to size with enough room for foliage expansion.

Avens
(*Geum Quellyon*)
Rose Family

The English seem to have the best luck with these cheerful flowers from Chile, witnessed by the fact that two of the prettiest cultivars grown were introduced from England nearly seventy-five years ago. Mrs. Bradshaw is a semi-double red and Lady Stratheden, a semi-double yellow. Those who succeed with geums adore them. The flowers suggest tiny 1½-inch roses. The foliage forms a handsome basal ruffle of a deep green, almost shiny texture. Flowers show off individually on wiry 2-foot stems through most of the summer. The roots have a spicy fragrance and were once used to flavor wine. Give geums a place in the sun and the best soil. Work in plenty of compost, add manure and some superphosphate. Set out nursery plants in spring or fall. Water deeply in dry spells. Clump in groups of 3 or 5 with a foot spacing between plants. Once established, and it may take a year or two, they will thrive. Geums can also be started from seed sown indoors in late winter for July bloom the first year or in midsummer for wintering over in a coldframe and bloom the following year. If geums have not wintered well in the past, try a light covering of clipped evergreen boughs after the soil starts to freeze. Divide plants every 4 or 5 years when blooms have faded.

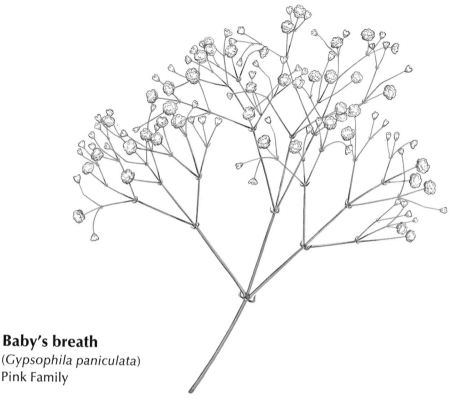

Baby's breath
(*Gypsophila paniculata*)
Pink Family

Dainty, misty, airy, feminine—all describe this gentle flower loved for filling-in border gaps and holes in flower arrangements. It is a bouffant plant with masses of tiny double flowers on wiry stems. A white coating on the lance-shaped leaves makes them appear gray. Consider it a permanent addition to the garden, for once settled in the plants form a rhizomelike taproot and they are difficult to move. Native to Central and eastern Europe, provide a sunny place where the soil drains well. Prepare it deeply and add a generous handful of lime for each plant. Mix it in well. Set out plants in spring and space them 3 feet apart. If the plant subsides in a few years, add lime again. Once established, the plants will need firm staking in late spring as they tend to be rank and floppy, especially after heavy rains. Save strong twigs from fall prunings or clip short several bamboo stakes and make a "fence" with strong twine. This 3-foot perennial will cover the supports by midsummer when it is in full bloom. If flowers are cut frequently, blooming goes on longer or it may spurt into rebloom in early fall. To dry the flowers, cut long stems just as the first flowers start to open. Hang in small bunches upside down to dry. The white double variety, Bristol Fairy, is handsome. There is also a pink one, equally lovely.

162

Balloon flower

(*Platycodon grandiflorus*)
Bellflower Family

The Greeks gave the name to this one—*platys kodon* or broad bell.
Balloon flower is a better name once the flower buds are formed. They
inflate, just like balloons, and split open to reveal the star-shaped,
2-inch bells of violet blue. There are also white and pink cultivars. Plants
are about 2 feet tall. The oval leaves are pleasing, leather textured and
deeply toothed. A dwarf form, *Mariesii,* is 18 inches tall. Flowering begins
in midsummer and continues until early fall. Excellent for cutting, but
sear the stem ends first before putting the flowers in water. Groom plants
often to remove faded flowers and prevent self-sowing. A good beginner's
perennial, once established, it remains for years and should not be disturbed. To achieve this long life provide a sandy, well-drained soil. Full
sun is best; light shade is a possibility, especially for the variety Shell
Pink. Space plants a foot apart. Plant in spring taking care to keep the
crown at soil level. Until you are sure of the exact location of balloon
flowers in the border, mark them with a label or stake after cutting the
tops in fall. They are late sprouters in spring. Many a novice gardener has
inadvertently dug up *platycodon* during spring clean-up.

Basket of gold
(*Aurinia saxatilis*)
Mustard Family

"Electric" gold upright clusters of these tiny rosette flowers challenge the muted tones of early spring bulb flowers so plan spring color schemes carefully. Also called gold dust, this one is an excellent plant to cascade over rock walls or poke out of their nooks and crannies. The foliage is hairy, gray toned, and semi-evergreen. A native of the Mediterranean region, particularly Turkey, it thrives if the soil is sandy or gritty and well drained. Full sun is best. As with candytuft, do not hesitate to discipline with clipping back after bloom. Even then, it may need to be divided every 3 or 4 years but be aware of the long tap root. Set out new plants in spring or fall and space them 1 foot apart. This one is also easy to start from seed.

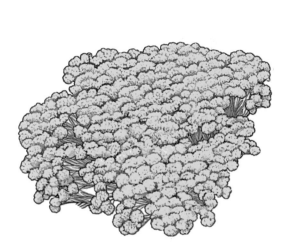

Beardtongue
(*Penstemon barbatus*)
Figwort Family

This exceptionally varied group of native North American plants could please an avid collector for a lifetime. This species deserves special mention as a border flower. Well-grown plants are 3 feet tall and bright with spikes of curious flowers that suggest foxgloves or gesneriad flowers. They are long rose-red tubes with two lips, the lower one bearded. The Latin comes from *pent stemon* meaning five stamens. The soft-textured linear leaves are opposite on the stems. Since these *penstemons* are found in the wild on forested slopes and moist meadows, this provides a clue for garden planting. They prefer sun or light shade, good drainage (otherwise they freeze out in winter), and moderate fertility. Plant them in spring, grouping them in the background with 18 inches between plants. When the soil is frozen, mulch carefully with evergreen boughs. Once established they should not need much attention. Divide only if they become crowded and fail to flower.

Beebalm

(*Monarda didyma*)
Mint Family

This casual and pleasant flower is especially at home in a country garden. A native of New England, it has been domesticated by hybridists and tamed into lovely cultivars. The centers of the blooms are whorls of skinny mint flowers surrounded by showy bracts making the whole flower look rather shaggy. Colors are pink, rose, scarlet, salmon, violet, or white and the bees do visit them frequently. The stems are typically square and the leaves rough textured. Most plants are 3 feet tall. Also known as Oswego tea, the entire plant is aromatic, and the leaves were once used for tea in Colonial times. Another name for the plant is horse mint. Grow it where the soil is moist, well drained, and fertile. Full sun is best, but light shade is tolerable. As with most mints, once established, their aggressive roots fan out. Divide every 3 or 4 years to keep under control and blooming well. The Latin name honors Nicholas Monardes, a sixteenth-century Spanish botanist and physician.

166

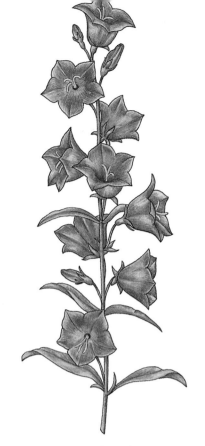

Bellflower
(*Campanula species*)
Bellflower Family

Bellflowers were favorites of Liberty Hyde Bailey who wrote a mono-
graph on them. There are nearly three hundred species distributed
throughout the North Temperate region but the majority of garden plants
are from the Mediterranean and from Central Europe. All of them are
characterized by upfacing bells in lavender-blue-purple shades or white
with basal tufts of spear-shaped foliage. Some are cunning low species
for rock gardens, others are upright for border flowers. Many are easily
grown from seed planted in summer for bloom the next year. Their
name is derived from the Latin for bell. The plants are most rewarding
for lazy gardeners as they are not too demanding of soil or location. Well-
drained average soil and a place in sun or light shade suits them. Be sure
to groom faded flowers to prevent seed pods, otherwise volunteer seedlings take over. Plant in spring, divide every third year, and cover with a
light mulch for winter. Some of the good garden species to try: C.
glomerata, a clustered type about a foot high with as many as twelve
bells in a bunch; Canterbury bells—C. *medium*—a biennial easy to grow
from seed; Carpathian harebell—C. *carpatica*—a cunning tuck-in plant
for rock gardens; peach-leaved bellflower—C. *persicifolia*—though its
foliage is more willowlike it has extraordinary, elegant, tall spikes to 3
feet lined with pretty upfacing bells.

167

Blanket flower

(*Gaillardia x grandiflora*)
Sunflower Family

This sunny summer flower should be more widely grown. Easy to raise from seed, it starts to flower in midsummer and keeps up until almost frost. A native North American wild flower which seedsmen have selected and bred for good growing habit and colors, it has all the sunny shades—gold, bronze, yellow, maroon, and cream—all mixed together in bright daisies. The leaves are long and linear with rough cat-tongue texture. Plants are 2 feet tall. Sow the seed in early spring and maybe they will flower late the first year. The soil must be light and well drained, and the site sunny. Dry spells do not discourage this one. But avoid planting where the soil is damp and poorly drained as the plants will not winter through. Once established, the root clumps can be lifted in late fall and used for root cuttings. Reset them at the same depth and plants will flourish in spring. Excellent as a cut flower; always groom faded blooms to prevent unwanted seed pods from forming. The Latin name honors Gaillard de Marentoneau, a French patron of botany.

Bleeding heart

(*Dicentra spectabilis*)
Fumitory Family

The plant explorer Robert Fortune brought this one back to England from Japan in 1847. The Greeks had a name for it, *dis kentron,* meaning two spurs. Rare is the perennial garden that doesn't have this old-fashioned flower and many youngsters equate it with the flowers at Grandmother's house. Everything about it is pleasing. The deeply cut, green, fernlike foliage, the graceful arching stems hung with the "bleeding hearts." Each flower is a heart-shaped pouch of rosy pink with a white tear hanging below. They pull apart easily to two equal halves. Grow *dicentras* in rich loamy soil in light shade. The 2-foot plants spread out in time and need at least 2-foot spacing, but choose the position carefully. The foliage and flowers are lovely in early spring but as soon as warm summer weather comes, the plants become dormant and disappear, leaving a gap. The flower and leaf stems are watery and the roots are brittle and difficult to plant. Small root divisions about 3 inches long are easiest to work with. Place them a few inches under the soil. Plant in early summer, right after bloom, or in early fall. Other species to consider are the plumy bleeding heart (*D. eximia*) or, for the wild flower garden, the native Dutchman's breeches and squirrel corn.

Candytuft
(*Iberis sempervirens*)
Mustard Family

Truly a plant for all seasons, this one is a delight in early spring when the clustered tufts of tiny white flowers bloom. Throughout the year it lives up to *"sempervirens"* (evergreen) with dark foliage reminiscent of yew. Candytuft looks elegant draped over a rock wall or forms a ground-hugging mat for edging. Never growing much more than 8 or 9 inches tall, it is tough and durable once established. It bears the classic name for Spain, Iberia, where several species are found. Do not hesitate to discipline candytuft by pruning right after bloom. Tolerant of light shade, it will also grow well in full sun, but it may be burned in sunny exposures if winters are open, with little snow cover. The browned leaves slough off when new growth begins in spring, or you can trim them off. Plant in spring or fall and set plants a foot apart. An annual form, *Iberis umbellata*, can be flowered from seed. Ideal for climates where summers are cool, plant it in the fall to bloom with later-flowering spring bulbs.

Christmas rose
(*Helleborus niger*)
Buttercup Family

In 1633 John Gerard recorded in *The Herbal* that hellebores "floureth about Christmasse, if the Winter be milde and warme." Somehow that schedule has remained down the centuries and the tradition became established. More realistically, the plant blooms in March where winters are severe and snow-covered and maybe in January or February where they are more mild. As to being a "rose" there is not even a family resemblance. This perennial is a challenge. It has handsome evergreen foliage that huddles together. Individual leaflets are long and deeply toothed but the overall effect is shiny and leathery. Plants are about a foot tall. Buds shoot up out of the ground on naked stems and open to a 3-inch-wide flower with five white petals and prominent yellow stamens. They fade to pink with age but remain white if cut and taken indoors. Just the right soil combination and a location in soft shade are vital necessities. Rich, woodsy loam is best, but work in compost, well-rotted manures, some bonemeal, and some sand if it seems heavy. Quick drainage is essential. Plant in spring, spacing about a foot apart. Notice the black roots which are poisonous if ingested. Water well in summer if dry and keep alert for slug invasions. Plants often need several years to settle down and bloom. Since the leaves are evergreen they are subject to winter sun and wind burn. Morning sun is usually best. When flowering does start, many a display has been saved from harsh winter winds or sudden ice or snow with a lath shelter over the plants. Once established, plants should not be disturbed. The Lenten rose (*H. orientalis*) blooms late in the season. Its leaves are larger and the flower fades to an unpleasant purple with age. These plants are not to be confused with the wild flower false or white hellebore (*Veratrum viride*) which also has poisonous roots.

171

Chrysanthemum

(*Chrysanthemum species*)
Sunflower Family

The Greeks named it *chrysos anthos*—gold flower. The Chinese have revered it for thousands of years and the Japanese have made it their national flower. Although the fall garden 'mums characterize this flower, the genus includes Shasta daisy, pyrethrum, Marguerites, and feverfew. There are nearly two hundred species and over three thousand cultivars. All have similar cultural needs. The fall flowering garden chrysanthemums are grouped under *C. x morifolium*. Plants range in size from 2 to 4 feet and flower types can be daisy, quilled, anemone, spoon, spider, pompon, button, and carnation. The best way to sort them out is to study catalogues and visit gardens and garden centers when they are in bloom. Plant 'mums where their display of color at the close of the growing season is an advantage—in window boxes, in terrace or dooryard tubs, massed in flower borders or along drives, and by split-rail fences. With care, colors combine with almost any color scheme and the choices are legion. Chrysanthemums are not for lazy gardeners as they need proper attention through the year. Buy rooted cuttings from reputable nurseries and set them out in full sun after the last frost. Soil must drain well and should be enriched with rotted manures, compost, and 5-10-5 fertilizer. Established clumps are lifted every spring when new shoots are several inches high. Pull off the younger, vigorous side shoots with sturdy pieces of root and discard the old centers. Keep varieties and colors separate. Allow at least 18 inches between plants, 2 feet for the taller ones. Water well after planting. Those who grow 'mums for shows feed plants on a monthly schedule until buds form. Maintain the plants well all summer. Keep beds free of weeds and water in dry spells. Unless 'mums are pinched back, they will grow skinny stalks and have few flowers. Pinching—taking out the terminal bud between thumb and forefinger—forces branching. Make the first pinch when the young plant is 6 to 8 inches tall. This will force the lateral breaks. When the laterals have grown another 5 or 6 inches, pinch all terminal buds again, leaving at least two leaves per stem. This may be enough to encourage a bushy plant. If not pinch

172

once again, but no pinching should be done after mid-July to allow
plants time to grow and set flower buds. 'Mums are susceptible to a
number of pests and diseases—aphids, spider mites, leaf hoppers, mildew,
rust, and leaf spot. The best cure is prevention: clean growing habits and
good air circulation around plants. Take quick remedial action if trouble
is spotted. When the flowering season is over cut the flower and leaf
stalks to a few inches above ground level. Although most of the outdoor
garden 'mums are quite hardy, winter mulch—either clean straw or salt
hay over the plants when the ground is frozen—helps. The florist's pot
'mums, forced for holiday and gift sale, are generally not winter-hardy
and usually are best discarded after flowering.

173

Columbine
(*Aquilegia x hybrida*)
Buttercup Family

Those who have seen the columbine, Colorado's state flower, in its natural Rocky Mountain habitat can understand the appeal of these flowers. Several hybrids which include this excellent species in their parentage have been developed for gardens. The 2- to 3-inch flowers grow in symmetrical sets of five. The five center petals are hollow and extend backwards to form long spurs. In between are five long petal-like sepals, usually of a contrasting color, to form a backdrop frame for the petals. These 2- to 3-foot-tall flowers are excellent for cutting and flourish if the soil is right: It should be enriched with humus to hold moisture but quick draining. Full sun is possible but light shade is better. The plants are easy to start from seed. Look for the McKana Hybrids or the Langdon Rainbow Hybrids. Both have wide color ranges of blue, pink, rose, red, purple, yellow, and white. Refrigerate seed for a week, then sow in midsummer for bloom the following year. Germination is slow—about 3 weeks. Transplant to a permanent place when the seedlings are large enough to handle. Columbines are often troubled by leaf miner which makes ugly tunnels in the leaves. Control with systemic sprays absorbed into the foliage. Plants tend to fade out in 2 years and should be replaced as the self-fed volunteers that can take over lack the vigor and characteristics of the true hybrids.

174

Coneflower
(*Rudbeckia fulgida*)
Sunflower Family

This cheerful wild flower comes from the Middle Atlantic States. Look for Goldsturm with gold-yellow daisies up to 3 inches wide or Gold Drop, a lighter-shaded double. Both plants are under 3 feet tall. Reliability is the coneflower. Plant it in average soil where is gets sun, or even a touch of shade, and it will reward with flowers from the middle of summer to late fall. The sunny-colored flower petals circle symmetrically around the high center cone of brown-black. Cut them often to encourage more. The plants tend to be rangy and the foliage is rough textured and sharply pointed at the tips. Bank coneflowers in casual borders or use them as landscape flowers for a naturalistic effect. Plant in spring and space individuals 18 inches apart. Divide every 3 years to keep them under control. A related species of great popularity is the gloriosa daisy (*R. hirta*) introduced in 1957. The flowers are huge, to 6 inches wide, some double and some bicolor in sunny golden shades. Plants are about 3 feet tall and often bloom the first year from spring-planted seed. A close cousin is the purple coneflower (*Echinacea purpurea*) which is a 3-foot-tall coneflower with maroon-pink petals and a high center cone. Flowers grow from midsummer to frost.

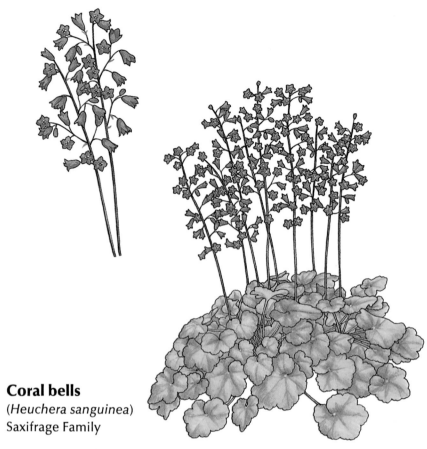

Coral bells
(*Heuchera sanguinea*)
Saxifrage Family

High praise goes to this excellent perennial. The leaves form mounds of shiny, semi-evergreen foliage suggesting rounded maple leaves. Elegant wiry spikes, about 2 feet tall, shoot up and are hung with tiny half-inch bells. Colors are lovely—pink, scarlet, coral, or white. Flowering continues through most of the summer. When massed in clumps, the flower spikes provide a pleasing airy quality. Coral bells tuck among rocks, too, and will grow in full sun or shade. Although a native species of the Southwest, its name honors Johann von Heucher, an eighteenth-century German botanist. Plant in spring, with 1-foot spacing, in well-drained soil. Be careful to keep the crowns just under soil level. Also, work around plants gently in spring when applying fertilizer, as they are shallow-rooted. In warmer climates, the foliage remains evergreen, but where winters are cold the leaves are subject to sunburn unless protected by snow cover or a light mulch. The mulch will also prevent heaving in spring thaws. Flowers last well when cut, but they are more elegant left as a garden display. Do cut off faded stalks to prevent seed pods. Clumps fill in rapidly and will need to be divided every 3 years or so.

Daylily
(*Hemerocallis species*)
Lily Family

With careful choice of hybrids long summer bloom can be achieved.
Sizes range from tiny 8-inch plants to 3-footers and flower colors spread
from palest yellows and creams to orange, gold, pinks, purples, near-
blues, and reds. Some are bicolored or mid-ribbed. Each lilylike flower
lasts but a day but there are always plenty of buds to keep color
coming along for weeks. In some warmer climates evergreen varieties
grow. Daylilies are undemanding. They do best in average soil if some
rotted manures and compost are worked in. Although experts advocate
at least 4 hours of sun for best bloom, the plants do well in shade.
Plant after flowering or in early spring or late summer. Space large
plants 18 inches apart, small ones closer. They grow from crowns—
where roots and stems meet—and this joint is placed about an inch
below the surface. The roots must be spread out in the planting hole.
Water well after planting and whenever there are dry spells. Feed
plants every spring with 5-10-10; too much nitrogen accentuates
foliage, not flowers. Slugs may be a problem but can be discouraged
with a ground mulch of wood ashes or sand. When clumps become thick
and bloom is less prolific, divide and thin. All parts of the plants are
edible, particularly the flowers, which are traditional in Chinese cooking.

Delphinium

(Delphinium elatum)
Buttercup Family

There is probably no more difficult flower to grow well than the delphinium, but the results are thrilling. They may grow to 6 feet tall in the most beautiful shades of blue imaginable, ranging from sky blue to navy blue, with variations in between such as lavender, mauve, purple, white, and even rose-red. Most flowers are 2 to 3 inches wide, some with double rows of petals. One sepal is spurred and the two tiny center petals form the "bee" or eye usually of a contrasting color. The foliage is elegant—palmate, deeply lobed and cut. Delphinium needs are specific: a long growing season with plenty of sun, cool nights, and good air circulation. The soil must be prepared deeply and allowed to settle before planting. Those who are expert often prepare the soil in fall and plant in spring. The ground needs plenty of well-rotted manures, compost, peat moss to hold moisture, plus sand to make it gritty. The pH reaction in the soil must be near neutral and liming is often necessary. Add plenty of superphospate and 5-10-10 fertilizer as delphiniums are big feeders. The planting surface needs a scratchy layer of wood ashes or sand on top to discourage slugs. When planting place the crowns at soil level and allow 2 feet, at least, between plants. Group them in clumps of 3 or 5 and place them strategically where their spires predominate. Water well with a ground soaker as overhead watering only encourages fungus problems such as black spot, crown rot, and mildew. A regular fungicide spray program is usually practical as a precaution. Stake when the flower spike starts to gain height to prevent it from snapping off in high winds or heavy rainstorms. When flowers fade, cut the stalk to the ground, feed again with 5-10-10, and water in dry spells to encourage rebloom in fall. Always remove faded bloom stalks to prevent seed pods and volunteer seedlings. There are many excellent cultivars to select, sold as rooted cuttings or true-to-seed strains, from reputable nurseries. To sow seed, refrigerate over night to break dormancy, then sow immediately, either in fall to winter over in a cold-frame, or indoors early in spring to set out later in settled weather. In some areas, delphiniums act like biennials and need replacing every few years. For winter care, cut stalks to the ground and remove faded and browned leaves. Place a light mulch of sand, pebbles, or wood ashes around the crowns to prevent rot. Cover with evergreen boughs or salt hay when the ground has frozen.

178

Evening primrose
(*Oenothera fruticosa*)
Evening Primrose Family

These native Northeastern U.S. plants have never become widely popular
as garden perennials perhaps because of their reputation for flowering
late in the day and fading the next morning. But if the day blooming
species called sundrops are chosen, the plants are quite appealing. Clump
them together in groups of 5 or 7 to make a good display. The blooms top
stiff 1½-foot stems and open their petals wide to form small cups.
Flowering lasts through midsummer. The leaves are thin and lancelike
and climb right up to the base of the flowers. Give plants a sunny place
where the soil is light and they will last for many years. This one is easy
to grow from collected seed. In particular, the strain *Youngi* has excellent
lemon-yellow color and good manners. Plant in spring or fall and allow
a foot between plants. Divide every few years to keep them vigorous and
feed when growth starts in spring.

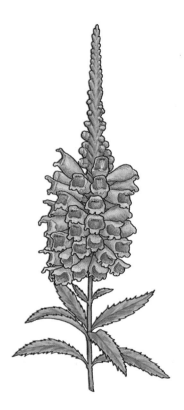

False dragonhead
(*Physostegia virginiana*)
Mint Family

These flowers have a slight resemblance to snapdragons. The 3-foot
spikes bloom late in summer and continue until frost. They have the
typical square stems of mints and the flowers are arranged symmetrically
around them, but if you want to rearrange them with a gentle push, they
will stay put. For this reason the plant is sometimes called obedience. A
wild flower of the Midwestern U.S., it can be found along riverbanks
and at woods' edge. A wild garden may be the best place to grow them
as they are aggressive and spread by underground stolons. They need
dividing every other year to be kept under control. Yet their lilac, rose,
pink, and white flowers lend a fine display to the late summer garden and
they are excellent for cutting. All they need is light shade, a cool moist
soil and room to spread. After the flowers fade, the calyx swells to form
a protective covering for the seeds within. Hence the Latin name from the
Greek *physa stege*—bladder covering. Seeds can be planted when ripe
for bloom the next season. Transplant to 18-inch spacing. Alternately,
root divisions take hold quickly in spring.

180

Flax
(Linum perenne)
Flax Family

For their magnificent chicory-blue color, flax flowers are forgiven if they last but a few days. More buds open the next day and the next all summer, if you cut spent flowering stalks to the ground. The inch-wide saucer flowers sit on airy panicles of wiry stems on plants 2 feet tall. Even the blue-gray, finely cut foliage is pleasing. This is an easy perennial to start from seed. Sow it early as soon as the ground can be worked and flowers may appear the first year, surely the next. Select a sunny place where the soil drains well. Plants self-sow readily once settled in. The garden perennial is a close cousin of the wild western-prairie flax. All have the typical flax family characteristics: five petals, five sepals, five stamens and five styles. *Linum* is the Latin name for flax, the source of linen, one of the earliest fibres used by man. The fabric is woven from the stem fibers of *L. usitatissimum* and the seeds are a source of linseed oil.

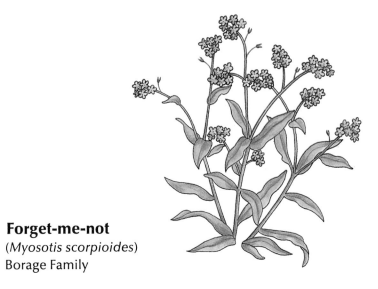

Forget-me-not
(*Myosotis scorpioides*)
Borage Family

Truly unforgettable is the color of this beguiling tiny flower with a yellow
eye. A cunning Old English name, Mouse Ear, refers to the slightly hairy
foliage which tends to be lance shaped. Although a native European
plant, forget-me-not has become naturalized in North America, especially
along streams and on moist woods' edges, a good clue for planting.
Provide a lightly shaded place where the soil is damp and cool. The
airy flowers will join the tulips for a lovely spring color display if the two
are companioned together. If the forget-me-nots take hold readily, they
will spread by stolonlike roots and also reseed themselves. They can
become a weedy nuisance, so be on the watch. Plants are easy to start
from seed sown in summer for spring bloom next year or from overgrown
clumps divided in fall. Flowering winds down with the coming of warm
weather and if the soil becomes too dry, the plants fade out entirely.
Where winters are severe, a light leaf mulch the first year or so will help
to carry them through.

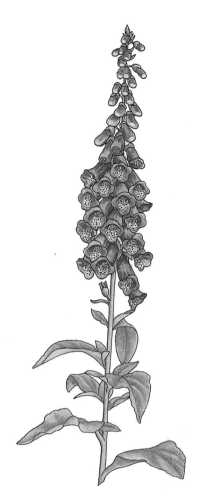

Foxglove
(*Digitalis purpurea*)
Figwort Family

It is no wonder that such an easy-to-grow flower is popular. Even the collar of ground-hugging, nearly foot-long leaves is handsome. Several spikes to 3 or 4 feet tall rise up, lined with lovely tubular flowers in shades of rose, pink, cream, and white. The open throats are usually spotted brown. Since this is a natural woodland flower, damp semi-shady locations suit it well although it will grow splendidly in a sunny border, too. Be sure the soil drains well as the thick roots rot in soggy soil. The foliage, which is persistent through winter, must also have good air circulation. Plant in spring and allow at least 2 feet between plants. They reseed easily and a thick clump is eventually formed. But since they are biennials, dividing is not necessary, usually, and once established the plants last for many years. Excelsior Hybrids have exceptionally fine flowers and are almost horizontal on the stem. For novelty, there is Foxy which blooms from seed the first year. The dried leaves, especially of pink-flowered varieties, are the chief source of the drug digitalis.

Gas plant
(*Dictamnus albus*)
Rue Family

A few perennials are so individual in appearance, they can be considered specimens to stand alone. This is one of them. From the ground up, it is handsome. The dark green compound leaves have a glossy sheen and, when rubbed, the volatile oils within give a citrus odor. In early summer, the plant blooms by sending up numerous airy spikes, to 3 feet in height, of starry white five-petal flowers with prominent stamens that curl upward. There is also a rose-pink variety. Glands on the flower spikes emit an oil or "gas." On a calm summer night, after the plant has been in bloom for several days, hold a match near the flowers and you will hear a puff or pop of the gas. Hence the name gas plant. A native plant throughout Southern Europe and Asia, right into China, it was said the ancient fire worshippers of India considered this a sacred plant. Provide well-drained fertile soil and an open airy site. Gas plant combines well with other perennials in a border or it serves well as a divider or specimen. It will tolerate light shade. Allow at least 2 feet between plants, 3 is better, for once in place it should not be disturbed for many years. If roots can be obtained for spring planting, they are better than seedlings which may take several years to bloom. The flowers last well when cut for bouquets, but allow a few to remain on the plant to form seed as they are splendid to dry for winter arrangements.

184

Geranium

(Geranium species)
Geranium Family

These "true" geraniums or cranesbills are hardy garden plants with gentle saucer-shaped flowers in soft pink tones. Each of the five petals is striped with rose lines. The foliage is deeply cut and beautiful as a groundcovering plant. Although they are in the same family as the house plant geraniums (*Pelargoniums*), these hardy wildlings bear no resemblance. There are over three hundred species throughout the temperate regions of the world, many of them wild flowers in this country. Several of the European species are excellent garden plants because they thrive in sun or light shade with little care. Most of the plants are low and spreading and need disciplining with a shears in summer or division every few years. Bloom is prolific in late spring with intermittent flowers until frost. The long-beaked seed capsule, suggesting a crane's bill, splits and curls open to release seeds. *Geranion* is the classical Greek name for crane. Plant in spring or fall and place in strategic locations either in rock gardens, along rock walls, or as an unusual groundcover. Add some compost and peat to the soil before planting. Some of the finest landscape species to look for are: *G. dalmaticum,* a cunning dwarf not over 6 inches tall with deep green foliage and sweet flowers; *G. ibericum,* a foot-tall plant with 2-inch near-violet flowers with purple stripes and handsome foliage; and *G. sanguineum,* which has several varieties, all of which have inch-wide flowers of palest pink and foliage which turns reddish in fall. This last species makes an excellent show plant for tucking into rock gardens or naturalistic plantings.

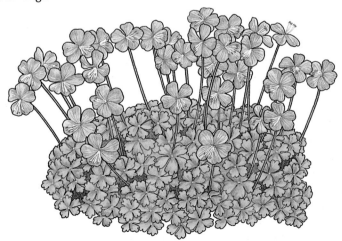

Golden marguerite

(*Anthemis tinctoria*)
Sunflower Family

A number of the chamomiles are used as medicinal herbs, but gardeners choose this species for its easy-to-grow flowers. The bright sunny daisies are 2 inches wide with flat center discs. Kelway has golden yellow petals while Moonlight is a softer lemon-yellow. Both plants grow about 2½ feet tall and the aromatic foliage is delicate and fernlike. Pinch some of it while you are working around the plants to smell it. This is an ideal daisy for lazy gardeners. Average soil is best and full sun ideal although it will tolerate a bit of shade. It is easy to start from seed sown in midsummer for bloom the following year. Or plants are available for spring planting. Cut the flowers often for bouquets; they will last a long time. Frequent cutting will also keep blooming up for most of the summer and prevent formation of seed pods. This one tends to self-sow and should be divided every 2 or 3 years to keep the plants vigorous. Though native to Central and Southern Europe, they have escaped and become naturalized in North America.

Hollyhock
(*Alcea rosea*)
Mallow Family

Technically a biennial, sometimes listed under annuals in seed catalogues, hollyhock self-sows so readily it seems a perennial. Tall and straight 6-foot stalks are lined with lovely wide flowers, either the hard-to-find singles or, more widely available, the over-ruffled doubles which have layers of petals making flowers up to 5 inches wide in cream, rose, pink, maroon, yellow, or purple. Leaves clump at the base and are large, round, crinkled, and hairy. Like snapdragons, hollyhock flowers open from the bottom bud upward until the whole spike is nearly in full bloom. When they fade, seed pods form. The place for hollyhocks is along a fence, by a garage wall, or in a sunny corner by the house. Average soil will do; fertile loam is better. Flowering lasts from midsummer to cool weather. Seed is available for the dwarf 2-foot cultivars such as Majorette as well as the 6-foot mixed doubles, Powderpuffs and Chaters. Seed sown outdoors in early spring might bloom by late summer the first year, but surely the second year. Nursery plants are also available in spring. Follow good clean-up practices in fall and cut down faded flower stalks to the ground, to prevent rust disease.

Iris

(Iris species)
Iris Family

These are truly regal flowers coming right after the tulips. All else in the garden pales beside them. There are so many colors, kinds, sizes, and seasons of bloom, the novice could be overwhelmed. Most iris grow from thick fleshy roots called rhizomes; a few are bulbous. All of them are monocots as are the grasses. The old-fashioned name for them is flag, but more romantic is fleur de lis. The Greeks named it for the goddess of the rainbow. Iris foliage grows in a fan with flat, soft green swords with a rubbery texture. The flowers have six petals. The upper three, called standards, form a huge cup, while the lower three, often bearded and called falls, hang downward like a skirt. The blends and contrasts of colors in these petals make the iris so spectacular. The only color missing is true red. The nearly two hundred species of plants range in the North Temperate regions of the world, many of them breeding stock for the garden cultivars now popular. Most gardeners choose the tall bearded iris, but, as their enthusiasm grows, the subgroups such as the Siberians, the elegant, wide-petaled Japanese iris for edges of ponds, and the cunning bulbous iris for early spring bloom also appeal. Iris need full sun, excellent drainage, and fertile light soil. They look best when given a place of their own in separate beds like roses, but they will companion well with other perennials. Proper planting and maintenance of the beds is crucial. Plant in summer after bloom when the rhizomes are easy to handle. Prepare the soil well in advance. To develop strong anchoring roots, low nitrogen and high phosphorus-potash fertilizers are good, either 5-10-10, superphosphate, or bonemeal. Go easy on manures and work in compost. The fat rhizomes lay flat. Roots grow from the bottom and leaves shoot up at right angles. Arrange the roots in groups of 5 or 7 with their points inward and the leaves outward. The foliage is often cut short in a fan about a foot tall, which makes planting easier, especially when dividing old clumps. Carefully scoop out a shallow area of soil so the roots can spread evenly on either side of the rhizome which rests on a tiny center mound of soil. Cover and pat firm. If a tiny bit of the top of the rhizome shows, that is okay, as they should be only an inch below the surface. The rhizomes multiply in time and every 3

or 4 years iris must be divided after bloom. Dig up the mat of rhizomes cut them apart, discarding the older centers and cutting out the stronger new roots with good eyes or buds. Rework the soil and start all over again with planting. The worst part: iris borer. This ubiquitous enemy is most destructive. It lives by gouging out rhizomes and can clean out iris in a summer or two. The moth lays eggs on old foliage in late summer. The eggs winter over to hatch and crawl into the leaves and down to the rhizomes. The best protection is good clean-up in fall, pulling up and carting away all old foliage, plus a second good clean-up in spring, pulling away any overlooked debris. Feed with 5-10-10 in spring. Systemic foliage sprays also help to protect the leaves from moths.

Leopards-bane
(Doronicum cordatum)
Sunflower Family

Though it seems to be stretching legends a bit, this perky sunny daisy was once believed capable of warding off dangerous beasts. A native of the Mediterranean region, its daisylike yellow flowers—up to 2 inches wide —with golden centers, are a delightful change of color and flower shape to blend with spring's tulips and primroses. Be careful when placing them that the flower colors are harmonious. The foliage is heart shaped and rough textured. Plants stand about 2 feet tall. This one has the peculiar habit of disappearing in summer so mark with a label where the plants exist lest they be dug up in fall when setting out hardy bulbs. Plant in loamy, moist soil in either full sun or light shade. Set them in groups of 3 or 5 with individuals a foot apart. Since they tend to grow thick mats of roots, divide every 3 years in later summer to keep them thriving.

Loosestrife
(*Lythrum Salicaria*)
Loosestrife Family

Those who have seen fields of this willow herb along river banks and in wet meadows may wonder why the plant needs a garden home. Yet some selections have been made from wild species and bred for good manners, color, and form. Some of the best work was done at the Canadian Agricultural Station in Morden, Manitoba and their introductions are the Morden Series. These plants have 3- to 4-foot spires of bloom. The flowers are circlets of tiny petals in pink, rose, and carmine red. The leaves are long and willowlike arranged in whorls around the stem. Loosestrife is a genuinely hardy plant ideal for giving height to a mixed border. Average soil suits it and it also thrives in low wet spots in full sun or light shade. Once established, it grows vigorously and must be divided every 3 or 4 years to be kept under control. Plant in spring or fall. This one is excellent for cutting and ideal for beekeepers since bees favor these flowers.

Lupine
(*Lupinus polphyllus*)
Pea Family

Lupines can be frustrating for many because their growing requirements are so specific. Cool growing seasons, well-drained soil that is slightly acid, and plenty of air circulation and sunshine. The lupines thrive in North America in the Pacific Northwest and in parts of New England. The 3-foot bloom spires are candles of color in summer bursting with pea-family flowers in blues, pinks, reds, bronzes, yellow, and white with many bicolors. The foliage is palmate, fingers of long, soft green leaves, hovering at the base. Seed of Russell hybrids is sold mixed or in separate colors. Plants are also available for spring planting. Soak seed overnight to soften the hard seed coat and plant in an outdoor nursery bed in midsummer. Move the seedlings when sturdy and large enough to handle, but, since they have a long taproot, disturb them as little as possible. Space plants about 2 feet apart and group them in clusters of 3 or 5. Add superphosphate or bonemeal but little nitrogen as they are legumes and obtain their own nitrogen. Water deeply in dry spells and remove faded flowers to prevent seed pods. Winter protection is recommended to prevent spring heaving. Advanced gardeners can root cuttings of lupines taken from early spring growth. Renew every few years.

Monkshood
(*Aconitum Napellus*)
Buttercup Family

In late summer leafy spikes 3 to 4 feet tall are trimmed with violet-blue granny's nightcaps, friar's caps, monkshoods or helmet flowers. Choose whatever name pleases for this European species. One can almost imagine faces peering out from under these curious hooded flowers. The glossy foliage is deeply cut and quite similar to that of delphinium. Monkshood is for judicious gardeners who will plant and grow it with caution because the leaves and roots contain a narcotic alkaloid, aconitine, which is poisonous if ingested. Even the Latin name is based on *akontion*, the Greek word for dart. The plants or roots are difficult to find at nurseries or in mail-order catalogues yet monkshood is one of the most dramatic choices for color display in shady, woodsy soil where it is cool and damp. It forms thickened roots which are best planted in fall, set just under the soil surface. Space them in clumps of 3 or so, 1 foot apart. Once established the plants should not be disturbed. Some winter protection around the thick color of leaves is practical for the first few winters until the plants are established. Sometimes the tall spikes become so heavy with leaves and flower buds, they need staking. Plants can also be started from fresh seed planted as soon as it is ripe.

Mountain bluet
(*Centaurea montana*)
Sunflower Family

This large shaggy perennial cornflower is a hardy import from Central Asia. Easy to grow from seed, it thrives in ordinary soil with little care. Plants are about 2 feet tall and densely foliaged. Initially leaves are woolly gray and develop into long lance shapes. The fat flower buds are rounded and the sepals outlined in black. They burst open to release shaggy 3-inch-wide daisies with loosely arranged long violet petals circling a darker purple center. They are excellent cut flowers, sometimes floppy; cut the early summer blooms often to encourage rebloom in early fall. A close cousin of bachelor button, it grows best in full sun but can tolerate some shade. This one spreads easily by stoloniferous roots. Keep after it and divide it at least every third year. Ripe seed is planted in summer for flowers the next year.

194

Oriental poppy
(*Papaver orientale*)
Poppy Family

Shimmering colors of crisp, crinkled petals distinguish these early summer saucerlike flowers. Shades range from red, orange, salmon, and lavender to white and bicolored, many with a dark basal spot. Flower stalks push up 3 feet tall from a cluster of deeply cut gray-green foliage. The only disadvantage of poppies is their short season of bloom in early summer. Thus, poppies should be companioned with later flowers such as baby's breath, asters, or phlox. Plant poppies in full sun or light shade. They need well-drained soil enriched with compost and rotted manures and fertilizer such as 5-10-5. Plant when dormant, usually in August. Poppies have long, rubbery tap roots and must have a deep planting hole. The crown is placed 3 inches under the soil surface and firmed in. Build a mound in the bottom of the planting hole, spread roots over it so the crown is at the right depth, half-fill, firm, and water. When it settles fill in the rest of the soil. In early fall new growth appears on new and established plants. Mulch these leaves with wood chips, pebbles, or pine needles to keep the crowns from rotting. If Oriental poppies become aggressive, thin them every 4 or 5 years. But dig deeply to get all the root, or broken pieces will remain in the soil and grow.

Peony
(Paeonia lactiflora)
Peony Family

Peonies are forever. Give them a good home and they will last for decades. In or out of bloom, these magnificent 3-foot plants can be used as hedges, specimens, or border complements. Fat round buds open to huge flowers, 6 inches wide or more, with masses of heavy petals in colors ranging from white, cream, pink, rose, or maroon to, most recently, yellow. The 3-part foliage is always appealing whether the plants are in or out of bloom. The Latin name is derived from Paeon, honoring a Greek physician who first used peonies medicinally. The Chinese have grown peonies for thousands of years and were the first to hybridize them. In English Tudor gardens they were called Chesses or Hundred-bladed Roses. The entire family comprises one genus with thirty-three species.

Most of the garden cultivators are derivatives of *P. lactiflora*. Numerous peonies are available for gardens and choices will depend on appeal and availability. Indicative of their long popularity, Festiva Maxima, introduced in 1851 remains one of the best cultivars available, a clean white fused with red petals. With proper selections, the peony flowering season can expand over 6 weeks by choosing early hybrids, tree peonies, Lutea, and midseason hybrids. The most popular are the doubles but of recent appeal are the single varieties. Planting is the most important phase of raising peonies. The best place is where the sun touches from late morning on or where there is light shade from high pruned trees. Allow 3 feet spacing between plants. Peonies are big feeders and need thorough soil preparation to last your lifetime. Plant from late September through October. Each peony needs a 2-foot-square hole of superb soil. To prepare it, dig out the soil and set it aside. Be sure the bottom of the hole is free of heavy stones. Mix with well-rotted manures, screened compost, a generous handful of limestone, and another generous handful of 5-10-5 fertilizer. Where soils are acid, avoid using peat moss at it will only accentuate acidity. If it is used, soak it first. Allow the soil to settle for a week before planting. Peony roots are long, thick tubers. Good quality ones should have 3 to 5 buds or eyes showing between the stumps of the old leaf-flower stalks. These eyes must be 1½ inches below the soil level, precisely. When setting the root in place, filter earth around with one hand while the other keeps the level accurate. Firm in and water. When the ground freezes hard, protect peonies the first winter with evergreen boughs, clean straw, or pine needles. In spring, remove the mulch, and, when new growth is several inches high, spray with a fungicide to discourage botrytis. Lightly scratch in a few tablespoonfuls of 5-10-5. To get huge flowers, remove the tiny pea-size side buds and allow one main central bud to grow. Ants often crawl around peony buds, attracted by the sweet exudation, but they are harmless. For cut flowers, pick peonies when the flowers are half way open. In describing peonies as cut flowers, Victoria Sackville-West described them as having "something of the cabbage rose's voluminous quality; and when it finally drops from the vase, it sheds its vast petticoats with a bump on the table." If peonies fail to bloom, they may have been planted too deeply, or in too deep shade; or they might be hungry, or victims of botrytis. In fall, as a precaution, always cut to the ground and haul away old foliage. Peony fanciers should also consider the glorious tree peonies (*P. suffruticosa*) called moutan by the Chinese. These are woody-stemmed plants that do not die to the ground. Their flowers are enormous with crinkled, crepe-paper petals in vivid colors. They bloom early, before the herbaceous peonies, and have the same cultural needs.

198

Phlox
(Phlox species)
Phlox Family

Phlox are the backbone of any perennial garden and it would be difficult to exclude them. And yet the stately stalwarts are but a suggestion of the vast variety in this family. There are phlox for shade, for groundcovers, for dangling over walls and hills, and for tucking in borders. They take their name from the Greek word for flame, a tribute to the color display in summer. Native North American plants, they have been carefully and beautifully selected and hybridized to provide some outstanding cultivars with good reputations for stamina. The best known are the perennial summer phlox, *P. paniculata,* with 3-foot-tall plants in a bright array of every color except yellow-gold. Some of them are bicolored with contrasting eyes, others are pure colors. Numerous cultivars are available. The leaves are opposite on the stems, oval with a sharp point. Each individual flower has five petals that open flat. They are fused into a long thin tube the botanists call salverform. The individual flowers form a bouquet on top of each stem. Summer phlox need full sun, fertile soil enriched with compost and 5-10-10, and plenty of water in summer. Don't neglect them in droughts. Plant in spring or fall and allow at least 18 inches between plants. Divide at least every 4 years and discard the old center. Be meticulous about cutting off faded flowers to prevent seed as the volunteers with ugly colors can take over! When summers are warm and humid, mildew can be a problem, turning leaves chalky white and weakening plants. Preventive sprays with fungicides in early summer help. So does good air circulation. To improve it, thin the spring shoots to 4 or 5 per root clump. And don't overlook these three phlox: moss pink (*P. subulata*), the flat mats of prickly foliage that burst with white, vivid rose-pink, or lavender flowers in early spring; wild sweet william (*P. divaricata*), which blooms somewhat later in shady nooks, with beautiful pale blue flowers on foot-high stems; and, close on its heels, *P. stolonifera,* an aggressive creeping groundcover which needs watching but which is redeemed by its lovely lavender-blue flowers.

199

Pinks

(*Dianthus species*)
Pink Family

The Greeks called them the divine flower or flower of Zeus. The English have grown them since the Norman conquest. The French raise them for their clove scent. The Americans tuck them in their rock gardens. The name of the family comes from the "pinked" edges of the petals, not the color. There are over three hundred species of pinks, most of them European and many of those diminutive alpines; probably ten percent are grown horticulturally. Choice depends on matching cultural requirements and garden design with species available locally or through mail-order. Pinks need full sun and a gritty, sandy, well-drained soil that is nearly neutral, cool growing seasons and mild winters. Where soils tend to be acid, include lime in the preparation for planting. Pinks are excellent tuck-ins and good edgers as many of them are dwarf. Colors are pink, rose, maroon, or white with single to semi-double flowers. The foliage tends toward gray-green and is rather grasslike. Pinks have a tendency to self-sow if faded blossoms are not cut back, resulting in a thick, overgrown clump. But if divided every few years and weeded several times a summer, they are a delight. Bloom is in early summer and if the weather is favorable, sporadic flowering will continue until hard frost. Especially appealing are the foot-tall *Alwoodii Hybrids* or cottage pinks (*D. plumarius*) and the 6-inch maiden pinks (*D. deltoides*). Many species can be grown from hardy seed which can be planted outdoors in the fall for flowering next year. Or cuttings taken in midsummer can be rooted in perlite and planted in late summer for next season's bloom. Protect where winters are severe with evergreen boughs. The florist carnations are hybrids of *D. carophyllus*.

Plantain lily
(*Hosta species*)
Lily Family

These are functional plants. They provide neat, formal borders of green or variegated foliage in shady places where little else can thrive. In midsummer, stiff stalks of lavender-blue bell-like flowers show off, but they are minor considerations; the leaves are the thing. There are nearly forty species of plants, all from the Far East—China, Japan, and Korea. Fanciers have a fascinating time sorting out their collective merits. Also known by another name, funkia, their Latin name honors Nicholaus Thomas Host, physician to the Emperor of Austria. All hosta leaves have deep ribs and heavy texture, some with very dark green colors, others with blue-gray, while still others have white margins or striations. Numerous species and cultivars are available and selections should be made on appeal. Those with blue-green leaves—often 2 feet long—can be grown in sun, but the variegated and heavily textured are best in shade. Plantain lilies grow from fibrous roots or rhizomes. Prepare the soil well before planting for, once established, that will be their permanent home, as they rarely need dividing and will discourage weeds. Don't neglect them in dry weather but drench them well. Hostas look best on long driveways, borders or shrub fringes but for a change of pace try a specimen plant or two among rocks. Slugs can be a nuisance and a scratchy layer of wood ashes or sand will discourage them. Mulch the first winter and work in superphosphate or 5-10-10 around each plant during spring cleanup.

Primroses

(Primula species)
Primrose Family

What happier choice of
blossoms to start a spring
garden than primoses?
Even the Latin name is rooted
in *primus*, the first. And
Shakespeare records in
The Two Noble Kinsmen:

"primrose, first born child of Ver,
Merry spring-time's harbinger."

It was the Bard who also first trod the "primrose path" in *Hamlet*. There
are so many choices—four hundred species—in this gracious family, that
cultural limitations will force the decisions. Primroses can be found wild
throughout the North Temperate zone. Some are hardy garden species,
others are tenderlings for greenhouses only. The professionals have
divided them into "sections" according to the flower type, and a good
number are for experts only. There are three good choices for the average
gardener. The most popular are the polyantha hybrids. Flower stems are
6 to 12 inches tall and florets are 1½ inches wide. The primrose of the
English wayside, *P. vulgaris*, has sweetly scented yellow flowers in early
spring. *P. japonica* is a candelabra type with tiers of flowers in whorls on
2-foot stems. Foliage of all primroses clusters in basal tufts around the
flower stem which is leafless. Flower colors have a wide range—white,
yellow, gold, orange, pink, red, maroon, blue, or purple. Provide
primroses with rich, loamy, woodsy soil enriched with compost, humus,
peat moss, and rotted manures. Choose a place in the shade, never full
sun, and have them near a source of water because they must never dry
out in summer. Give them a light feeding after bloom to strengthen the
plants. And when the clump becomes thick and overgrown, divide a week
or two after flowering, every 3 or 4 years. Red spiders can be a nuisance
if the summers are dry and hot. Keep plants moist and mist the foliage to
deter them. Primroses are easy to raise from seed. Freeze it first for 48
hours and plant immediately. Start seedlings indoors, in late winter or in
midsummer. Space young plants about 6 inches apart. Although the
plants are winter hardy, tuck them in with a salt hay or straw mulch
when the ground freezes to prevent heaving in spring thaws.

Rock cress

(*Arabis caucasica*)
Mustard Family

A good flowering companion for spring bulbs, this gently fragrant plant deserves more opportunity. It comes from the Mediterranean region as far east as Arabia and Iran, which provides a cultural clue: sandy, well-drained soils and sunny exposure. Rock cress tucks into garden walls; tumbles in rock gardens; and carpets tulips, pansies, or hyacinths in bloom. The plant forms a basal ruff of wide, woolly, soft-textured gray leaves, about 3 inches long. The early white blooms push up on little stiff stalks to form short racemes. The single ones have four petals to form a symmetrical ½-inch flower. The double, *Flore Pleno*, which is much preferred, has a longer season than the single. Rarely over 9 inches tall, the plants need disciplining after bloom to keep them in bounds. Plant in early spring, or better, after bloom, if a neighbor is dividing overgrown clumps. Allow 9 inches between plants. Where winters tend to be open without protection of snow cover, a light winter mulch will help to carry the plants over. Even with cutting back, plants may need dividing every 3 or 4 years.

Sea pink

(*Armeria maritima*)
Leadwort Family

If a plant could be called cunning, this one surely is. At home on the
Mediterranean shores in North Africa and Europe, it thrives where the
soil is light and sandy, in full sun. Reminiscent of chives in bloom, this
one forms clumps of blue-gray, evergreen, grasslike foliage. In late spring
and early summer, the ball-like blossoms shoot up on bare stalks, just
under a foot tall. The prettiest is a red-pink, although there is also a white.
Sometimes called thrift, these flowers can be cut and hung upside down
to dry if picked just before they are fully open. Plant in spring and use
as a tuck-in around rocks or as a delightful edging. Sea pinks are also
excellent for shore gardens. The center tends to die out in a few years.
Divide every 2 or 3 years in spring to keep them flourishing.

Sneezeweed
(*Helenium autumnale*)
Sunflower Family

This native North American plant is sometimes called Helen's flower. It does not make you sneeze although Indians were believed to use it as an errhine. It blooms in late summer and introduces the lovely fall colors, preceding the autumn foliage display and the chrysanthemums by a month. The 2-inch daisies with bronze, maroon, yellow, and gold tones have flat central discs. Plants are tall and rangy, to 4 feet, and need staking to keep them from being floppy. Leaves are about 4 inches long and lance shaped, with saw-toothed edges. As with most members of this clan, a place in the sun where the soil drains well is best. Plant in spring with 18 inches between plants. Divide every 2 years to keep under control and cut flowers frequently for bouquets.

Speedwell
(*Veronica species*)
Figwort Family

This varied group of plants ranges from a tiny nuisance lawn weed to elegantly spired border flowers. The showy spikes offer some of the finest blues for the garden, from early summer until almost frost. All *Veronicas* thrive in average soil that drains well. Full sun is best but they will tolerate some shade. The spikes of bloom are a mass of tiny saucer-shaped flowers and prominent stamens, and the stiff stalks are trimmed with sharply pointed leaves. Plant in spring or fall and allow at least 18 inches between plants. To be sure they are securely settled the first winter, use clean straw mulch or evergreen boughs over the plants. Once established, do not disturb unless they become aggressive; then divide. Groom faded stalks after bloom to prevent seed pods. Here are some of the best cultivars: *V. incana,* a Russian species, has woolly leaves and early flowers on foot-high plants; *V. latifolia* from Hungary has superb blue color on 2-foot spikes for midseason bloom; *V. spicata,* Blue Peter, is 18 inches high and prolific with multi-stemmed plants; and *V. longifolia subsessilis* is a real background plant, 2 feet tall, for late summer bloom. This one may need staking.

206

Stokes' aster
(*Stokesia laevis*)
Sunflower Family

This big cornflower is a delight for flower arrangers. It lasts well when cut and combines well with a number of flowers. It bears the name of Dr. Jonathan Stokes, a nineteenth-century English botanist. One reason this lovely flower is not more widely grown, is that it is not trustworthy where winters are severe and often freezes out. Also, it is a late bloomer. In the southwestern U.S., this rare, wild Stokes' aster is found in pineland forests along the coast, a vital clue to success. Grow where the soil drains well, in full sun, and provide winter protection with evergreen boughs after the soil is chilled. Several improved cultivated varieties are available, including a white one, but the blues are prettiest. Plants average 18 inches in height. Flowers may be up to 5 inches wide. The center petals are tubed and the outer background petals spread wide and flat. Leaves are long, spear-shaped, and shiny. Plant in spring with 1-foot spacing between plants. Divide established clumps every 3 years. Relatively trouble-free, it is also easy to start from seed sown in midsummer for bloom the following year.

Sunflower

(Helianthus decapetalus v. multiflorus)
Sunflower Family

The thinleaf perennial sunflower is a close cousin of the common annual as well as of Jerusalem artichoke. With the swing to naturalistic landscaping, this is an excellent choice for big properties. A native North American plant, it likes to spread out to 4-foot heights and take over. But when it blooms in late summer, and the stems are topped with yellow, 3-inch dahlialike flowers, its coarseness is forgiven. They are excellent teamed with asters. The foliage is coarse and deeply toothed and the stems are stiff. Roots grow deep and are fibrous giving them a strong hold once established. Plants are easy to start from seed sown in summer for bloom the next year. Or divisions can be planted in spring. Other than a sunny site and average soil, the plants need little attention. In humid summers, mildew can be a problem and the leaves become coated with gray mold. Flowers are excellent for cutting, and the more they are cut, the more they keep coming. Divide every other year to keep under control.

208

Tickseed
(*Coreopsis lanceolata*)
Sunflower Family

Here is the ideal summer daisy for beginners. A wildflower of the
midwestern U.S., domesticated by seedmen who have selected special
strains for gardens, its name comes from the Greek *koris,* a bug, and
opsis, like, because the seeds were thought to resemble a bug or tick.
Well-grown plants are about 2 feet tall and the yellow daisies are about
2 inches wide. They may suggest black-eyed susans or gloriosa daisies
since many of them have dark centers. The lance-shaped leaves are fuller
at the base and sparser as the long, wiry flower stems grow upward. The
daisy can become floppy and self-sows easily if flowers are not cut often
for bouquets or removed when faded. Flowering continues through most
of the summer if the spot suits them: full sun, light, well-drained soil,
not overly fertile. This one is easy to start from seed sown in late summer
for bloom the next season. Space plants a foot or so apart. A tall rangy
annual, *C. tinctoria,* with yellow, red, and mahogany flowers is called
calliopsis.

Tufted pansy
(*Viola cornuta*)
Violet Family

Think of these perky plants from Spain as hardy pansies without any faces. The flowers are smaller than pansies—to 1½ inches—and have a tuft or horn on the back. Colors are solid in shades of lavender-blue, velvet purple, apricot, rose, or white. The foliage is more oval than heart shaped and plants are about 8 inches tall. They flower early in spring, with the spring bulbs and primroses, and make good companions for them. Their flowering will last for a long season if old flowers are groomed promptly after fading and if the summer heat comes gradually. Tuck in rock gardens, between clumps of bulbs, or use as edgers in a border. Light shade or sun suits them and the soil should be moist and well endowed with humus and compost. Sow seeds in late summer and winter them over in a coldframe or protected nursery bed. Replant to their permanent places as soon as the ground is workable. They last for many years and spread by thick roots if watered well in dry spells and fed after bloom with 5-10-10 fertilizer. If they become thick and overwhelming, divide after bloom and separate to individual plants. Be sure to keep the crowns at the same planting depth.

Yarrow

(*Achillea species*)
Composite Family

Achilles is said to have used this plant as a styptic for his Greek soldiers
in the Trojan Wars. A remarkably accommodating flower, it needs little
care and provides color from early summer to cool fall weather. Give it
a place in the sun, high and dry, preferably where the soil drains well with
plenty of airy space to show off the ferny foliage. Although there are
several kinds of yarrow, from cunning, spreading, rock-garden species
to the border stalwarts, two are liked best. *A. ptarmica*—especially The
Pearl, which has rounded, double, pear-like white flowers ideal for
bouquets—is almost 2 feet tall. This one was once called Old Man's
Pepper as the roots were used for snuff (*ptarmica* is from the Greek for
sneezmaking). *A. filipendulina*—particularly Moonshine—is handsome
with flat-topped yellow flowers on 2-foot stems. The foliage is silver-gray
and fernlike, and the flowers are excellent for drying. This one resembles
the white, wild yarrow of the fields. Although a wine-colored cultivar of
the wildling is available, it has the aggressiveness of a weed and can
become a nuisance. Plant in spring or fall, space 18 inches apart, and cut
faded flowers promptly after bloom. Divide every 3 years to keep
flourishing and under control.

211

6. shade

A change is taking place in the suburbs; they are maturing. Houses built in the postwar years are growing older. Saplings planted to provide shelter have become forests. Hedges, little shrubs, and cunning landscape plants meant to tuck homes in are in many cases engulfing them.

This proliferation of foliage presents a challenge for gardeners—shade. It is an environment that bewilders many. Yet nature "plants" in shade all the time. Many of the earth's loveliest flowers thrive in woodlands where the sun barely touches. An understanding of the character of shade and the particular attention needed for plants growing there will make all the difference. A shady garden can be one of the pleasantest places. It is cool in summer, and the subtleties of foliage can be delightful elements of your design.

The factor of coolness is often overlooked when planning shade environments. Yet it permits many plants to grow that otherwise might be baked right out of existence. The early spring wild flowers are a typical example. They need a sheltered home. Consider how many ferns colonize the woodland floor. Many of the handsomest woody plants—laurel, azaleas, rhododendrons—need the shelter of shade to succeed.

Your garden does not have uniform shade all through the year. It varies in intensity. The ideal way to approach shade is to observe its patterns for twelve months before doing any major garden planning. The available light changes with the seasons. In spring and winter when there are no leaves on the trees, the light is much brighter than in summer and fall when there is a foliage canopy. The sun moves differently with the seasons. In winter, when it is lower on the horizon, late to rise and early to set, the quality of sunlight is less intense than in summer. Areas of the garden that are sunny in spring and winter may be completely shaded in summer and fall. Knowing these light and shade patterns will make a difference to the success of your garden.

Deep Shade

Deep shade is where there is no hint of sunlight for any part of the day. Beech and maple trees, especially, create this type of shade. Rather than fight it and force plants to eke out a meager existence, join it and follow what the landscape experts have learned—groundcovers are the best solution. Three excellent ones, though ubiquitous, serve well. These are pachysandra, myrtle, and ivy. All of them are evergreen, inexpensive, and quick to establish. Once in place, these groundcovers are practically maintenance free. They will spread quickly, fill in, and last almost forever. Local nurseries may suggest other suitable plants.

Astilbe's feathery spikes are a delight in shady nooks.

Impatiens and coleus are a reliable team where there is little sun.

214

Full Shade

The canopy of tree foliage provides full shade in nature. The density of this cover varies with the kinds of trees. Oaks will provide a denser shade than such open-leaved trees as locusts. Lindens are denser than ashes. Sometimes shade trees can be pruned high so their lower branches are eliminated to lift the shade cover and allow some light to penetrate. These same trees can also be thinned out from time to time to keep the branching from becoming too dense and closing out light as the trees thicken and grow.

Full shade can also be found on the north side of buildings where the sun never touches. Or pockets between buildings and fences can shut out light for the greater part of the day.

Half Shade

This environment does receive some sun for a part of the day, either as the low morning sun gently wakes the day or when it appears to slip off the earth at dusk. This quality of light is easier on plants than the brunt of the high-noon sun and is sufficient for a great number of flowers. Many actually prefer this kind of environment. Three to four hours of sunlight on either side of the noon hour qualify for half shade.

Light Shade

These are the places where there is good-quality light for most of the day. It is bright all day long with shafts of sunlight piercing through. High-pruned trees provide light shade, as will some of the smaller landscape trees such as dogwoods and crabapples. This is the least difficult of all shade categories and allows the widest selection of plants. Many sun-loving flowers grow quite well in these sites.

What to Grow in Shade

Planning for shade should include shrubs, ferns, and hardy bulbs as well as flowers. They will provide the background, flower color, and foliage diversity needed for the year-round scheme. Without representation from all of these plants, the shade garden would be very meager indeed.

Among the shrubs that do exceedingly well in shade are azaleas, rhododendrons, and laurels, plus many local woodland species. Abelia is a dainty charmer for late summer bloom. Witchhazels and enkianthus can also be selected but are large bulky plants that need space.

Ferns are natural shade plants. Local species from nurseries or nearby mail-order houses are the best sources. You may prefer to visit gardens where ferns are growing to select those which appear most suitable.

Spring bulbs are a splendid source of color for springtime from the earliest crocus to the daffodils and late-flowering tulips, with assorted minis and species in between. Garden centers and mail-order catalogues supply them from September on, when the bulb-planting season is at its height.

Flowers—both annuals and perennials—should coordinate with these other plants in season of bloom, foliage texture, and floral color. The main thrust of shade-tolerant herba-

A fine perennial border in a shady nook is well worth the effort where lilies, phlox, astilbes, impatiens and artemisia can blend.

ceous plant bloom is in spring. This includes a generous assortment of wild flowers. The perennials can carry the transition into summer, while shade tolerant annuals have to take over for color in full summer. In fall, the tree and shrub foliage takes over as it changes from its cooling green to the vibrancy of autumn colors.

Here are some of the perennials and annuals that will tolerate shade. Full shade accommodates many spring wild flowers, which are included, and several handsome groundcovers.

FULL SHADE

Annuals

Impatiens

Perennials

Barrenwort	Hosta
(*Epimedium*)	Lamium
Bugle (*Ajuga*)	Mint (*Mentha*)
Bunchberry	Oconee bells
(*Cornus canadensis*)	(*Shortia*)
Ginger (*Asarum*)	Phlox
Goutweed	Trillium
(*Aegopodium*)	Virginia bluebells
Hepatica	(*Mertensia*)

HALF TO LIGHT SHADE

Annuals

Ageratum	Impatiens
Alyssum	Lobelia
Begonia	Pansy
Coleus	Torenia
Flowering tobacco	Vinca

Perennials

Aster	Golden star
Astilbe	(*Chrysogonum*)
Balloon flower	Lily turf (*Liriope*)
(*Platycodon*)	Leopards-bane
Bleeding heart	(*Doronicum*)
(*Dicentra*)	Monarda
Campanula	Monkshood
Candytuft (*Iberis*)	(*Aconitum*)
Columbine	Peony
(*Aquilegia*)	Phlox
Coral bells (*Heuchera*)	Primrose (*Primula*)
Daylily (*Heuchera*)	Sedums
Foxgloves (*Digitalis*)	Speedwell (*Veronica*)
Forget-me-not	Sweet woodruff
(*Myosotis*)	(*Asperula*)
Geranium	Viola

Planting

There can be no bypassing of soil preparation for the shady garden. It is essential, for the plants will need all the help they can get. It might be assumed that soil underneath the shade trees will contain a natural accumulation of humus. This may not always be true. Check the soil—deep down. Spade it in areas where the garden is planned and see if it has a humusy content. If it does, the soil will be soft-textured and look dark and fibrous. It should also have an earthy, mossy odor.

If in doubt, it never harms to add humus. The addition of leafmold, weathered manures, peat moss, or compost will increase the vibrancy of the soil and add to its water-holding capacity. The soil that can be expected to have any reasonable humus content is true woods soil where a new residential property has been carved out of a woodland region. Such soil may need the addition of builder's sand to lighten it and make it easier to work and plant.

All shade-garden soil should be enriched with fertilizer. A well-balanced chemical fertilizer such as 5-10-5 is fine, or you can use the organic sources such as bloodmeal; wood ashes are good. Follow package label instructions. The pH reading will be important, as tree leaves tend to make soil more acid. If planting plans lean toward natural woodland wild flowers, a reading somewhere between 5 and 6 would suit a number of plants. A simple pH test can be made with a home kit, but be sure to take accurate samplings from several locations. If the soil is too acid, applications of ground limestone will help to correct this. Proportions are supplied on the bag or provided by the test kit.

Dig the soil several weeks in advance of planting. This will allow time for the soil to settle and reveal humps or low-lying areas where rainfall drains poorly and causes puddles. As with the flower borders, the shade planting needs to be thought out and planned on graph paper. Since the plants suited for shade have special times of year when they are best planted, spaces will have to be left in the ground for future plantings. If planting in spring, spaces for fall-planted bulbs or perennials could be filled in with shade annuals.

One caution when planting in shade: allow wider spacing than you would in a sunny area. One of the biggest problems in shade is poor air circulation. Sometimes on warm sultry summer days the humidity hangs in there and mildew-fungus problems abound. Allow wider spaces between plants and aim for greater variation in foliage textures. With heavy-foliaged plants, such as hostas and daylilies, include ferns or even woody plants such as azaleas or rhododendrons to provide some ground level space for air movement.

The MFW System

Once the shade garden is planted, that will not be the end but the beginning of its tending. Shade gardens do best by following that MFW system, that is, mulch-feed-water. It works well because the shade garden has some special maintenance problems.

The obvious mulch for shade is the leaf mulch—either the chipped leaf mulch described on page 86 or your own compost leafmold that is available. Sometimes the finer bark chips work well. The mulch should be at least 2 inches deep; 3 inches is better. The layer will keep down weed growth, keep roots cool, and help to maintain the soil moisture.

Feeding is especially important in shade. Shade-tree roots are gluttonous and usurp enormous quantities of nutrients from the soil. The shrubs, ferns, bulbs, annuals, wild flowers, and perennials that grow beneath them are in a constant contest for soil nutrients and, unless additional is provided, the trees win.

Shade gardens will need to be fed every spring with a full application of 5-10-5 or a similar formula. The easiest way to apply this is when you are on your inspection tour, checking over how the garden survived the winter. With mulches removed you will be able to observe the plants closely and pull off any winter debris. When the soil is dried out, you can lightly scratch in some fertilizer.

Then, as the summer progresses, watch how the plants are thriving. If their color pales or if bloom was less than it has been in past years, an additional application of superphosphate may be needed. This is the fertilizer with the high middle number, 0-20-0, which promotes flowers and sturdy roots.

Shade gardeners may forget that the leaves overhead are often umbrellas. While summer showers may do very nicely in keeping the lawn well watered, shade-tree leaves shield the ground directly underneath and few drops touch the soil. If this seems hard to believe, go out and feel the soil in a shady area sometime after a summer shower. You will probably be quite surprised to find how little water actually penetrates. It takes a good steady downpour to soak the ground under shade trees.

Watering is essential, therefore. Soil-soakers, either the canvas type or the perforated plastic hoses, are the best because they will keep the foliage dry. Watering this way will not add to mildew-fungus problems. Or, if fussy, thirsty plants need coddling, the good old-fashioned watering can with the spray head removed will suffice.

7. planting in special places

How splendid it would be if there were solid rules for growing flowers anywhere. But there are not and we are challenged to grow them in unusual places and use them in unusual ways. Special places need special consideration, and special uses need special knowledge.

Gathered here are some of these specialties that will expand the dimensions of flower gardening.

City Terrace

The city gardener has several advantages over his country cousin. His flowers are close at hand: He simply steps across the threshold and there is the garden. The greenery can often be seen from a living room, dining room, kitchen, or bedroom, wherever the terrace borders. Color schemes can be extensions of the interior decor.

City gardeners can often complete their tending chores in the cool hours of the morning and then be ready for relaxation while the country cousins may just be half way through

225

their day's chores, for there is yet a lawn to mow and a vegetable garden to weed.

In the city, soil can be created by following the right recipe for an ideal growing foundation. Although the city gardener may find this is initially the hardest part of getting started— the hauling and mixing—once the terrace garden is going, the upkeep of the soil is relatively easy.

The city terrace gardener has some difficulties that the country cousins never endure. These are the forces of the elements—high winds, intolerable heat reflected from buildings, soot, and polluted air. These factors put limits on flower-growing possibilities and make the daily upkeep of the terrace garden essential. One day's neglect in the brunt of summer heat can be disastrous.

Despite certain limitations, balconies do offer some possibilities for growing plants. The light is often limited because the balcony above shades the balcony below, but nonetheless it is an opportunity to cultivate your own garden in the city which should not be missed. More flexible are the larger terraces of the top-floor penthouses or the lower-level rooftops. Gardens on small balconies have to be made exclusively in containers with drain saucers of some kind, either built-in metal trays on the floor to accommodate gravel and pebbles, or pots, tubs, and jardinieres with individual saucers. If these drainage provisions are not made, neighbors below will be drenched every time you water the plants.

Larger terraces and penthouses will have parapets and can have built-in planters made of cement, brick, or concrete blocks. But before this type of garden gets too far into the planning-cost stages, check the local city building codes and ask the building manage-

Lantana, marigolds, petunias, and salvia are among the sunny flowers that will thrive in the baking heat of a city terrace.

ment for regulations. Some of the older buildings may not support the heavy weight of built-in planters. In addition, there could be serious problems of drainage and seepage.

Since built-in planters are relatively expensive, if you don't plan to stay long you should consider instead a portable garden of attractive tubs, pots, barrels, and terra-cotta jardinieres. In fact, this sort of garden has more charm if the containers have some character. I have seen a most charming city terrace garden made with a collection of old wooden pickle barrels, maple sap buckets, and soy tubs. They were left in their natural wood color and arranged in corners and all along the side of the terrace. Stuffed with assorted summer annuals and draped with ivy and vinca, the pots and the flowers were a constant source of color.

Pot size is important for a city terrace planting. The smaller the container, the more quickly it will dry out. Although dozens of small 5- or 6-inch pots might seem like an easy design concept, they would be a nuisance to water as they would dry out in a few hours' time in the heat of the day. A city terrace planter, no matter whether it is a pot, a tub, or a planter box, should be at least 12 inches deep. This will provide good root space and allow enough soil moisture to be retained for proper growth.

Containers abound these days. Even department stores carry assortments of weatherproof garden planters that are attractive and durable. Some of the newer plastic tubs and imported clay and terra-cotta pottery from Italy and Mexico are handsome. Use your imagination when selecting containers. As long as there are drainage holes for excess water to run off, almost anything goes.

228

Soil is the most important part of the city garden. It must be lightweight, yet heavy enough to support and anchor roots in high winds. It must also be fertile and water-retentive. To achieve these qualities you will have to mix your own. The hardest part will be transporting the ingredients up in the elevator, trip by trip, until all the materials are gathered together. If there are a number of containers to fill, a plastic garbage can makes a good mixing bowl, if you have space for it. Or you can mix the ingredients on the floor of the terrace and clean up afterward.

Philip Truex, who wrote *The City Gardener,* offered his container-soil recipe more than fifteen years ago. It is still an excellent one to follow today. He recommends that for each 25 pounds of topsoil, you add 10 pounds of leafmold, compost, or humus, 2 quarts of peat moss, and 2 quarts of vermiculite, horticultural grade. To this add a handful of superphosphate and another handful of dried cow manure.

This basic recipe provides a soil that drains well and retains moisture. However, as with all container gardens, regular feeding with a water-soluble fertilizer should not be neglected. Most terrace gardeners use a fertilizer every week or two at quarter-rate dilution, depending on how well the plants are growing and their flowering response. Too much feeding can promote lush leaf growth and no flowers. Insufficient feeding can result in slow growth.

Since drainage is so essential in a terrace garden, a deep drainage layer should be put in the bottom of each container first, before it is filled with soil. Even though there are drainage holes (and drill them if they aren't there), the drainage layer will provide that extra insurance that excess water will run off easily. If not, the roots become weak and may even rot if kept soggy.

One of the easiest drainage materials to obtain is cat-box filler. Put a 2-inch layer in the bottom and lay a wire mesh screening on top of it so the soil does not leach through it. Or gravel, pebbles, even plastic packing "noodles," are good, but always lay the mesh or sphagnum moss on top before placing the soil layer so it does not leach out.

Summer annuals do splendidly on the city terrace. In the city you will want flowers as soon as you can get them. Seeds take much too long to amount to anything. Flats of seedlings abound in the city in spring. Local grocers have flats of herbs and annuals to sell, as do the dime stores and the corner plant stores.

Petunias, marigolds, zinnias, verbena, sweet alyssum, geraniums, and ageratum do splendidly. Where there is less sun, try impatiens, begonias, and dwarf flowering tobacco. Use vinca and ivy to trim the boxes. Lantana does well but beware of white fly. Once it gets a start on the terrace it is difficult to control and lantana is a favorite host plant.

Perennials can also be grown in the city but they do cause problems in that they are rather "permanent." There is little opportunity to change plantings from year to year and if you want to plant bulbs in the fall for spring bloom, the roots of the perennials in the confines of the boxes don't allow much room for bulbs too. Nonetheless, you might like to try a few for their texture and color. Some of the best are gaillardia, columbine, summer phlox (it doesn't get too tall), iberis for its evergreen foliage, and coral bells. Don't forget vines such as morning glory and moonflower.

Once the city terrace garden is planted,

check it daily. It will probably need watering every morning. Also, hose the foliage to wash off the evening's accumulation of soot. No rigid schedule can be set for feeding the plants —you will have to be the judge of how the plants are responding in growth and bloom. Clip faded flowers promptly to keep blooms coming and if the plants become leggy and floppy, don't hesitate to cut them back. They will grow back quickly and bloom longer.

Cutting Garden

The cutting garden is rare today because most suburban gardeners do not have the growing space in a sunny portion of the yard to devote to flowers for bouquets only. Flowers lopped off at their peak display period can void the garden of color.

Those homeowners who have a passion for arranging flowers indoors all spring and summer find the cutting garden a necessity and not a luxury. Also, those who are keen on competitive flower arranging or on drying flowers for fall and winter bouquets find special pleasure in experimenting with unusual blooms for arrangements and drying.

Since the point of the cutting garden is maximum production of flowers, it should be located where the plants will receive sun at least 7 or 8 hours a day. This is the same requirement that vegetables need, so perhaps the vegetable garden can spare a few extra feet. Flowers, as well as vegetables, benefit from maximum sunlight if the rows are located on east-west lines. Put the tallest flowers to the north. As the sun lowers in late summer, the taller plants will not shade the shorter ones.

There are ample selections from both annuals and perennials for cutting. If space is at a premium, the perennial cutting flowers can be grown as part of the landscape plan in other places. For example, peonies can form a handsome property hedge and, if grown in quantity, they will provide plenty of flowers for both display and cutting. The same is true for iris and roses.

Or you can compromise. If annuals are your favorites for cutting, the allotted sunny space can be devoted to them and you can tuck in a few favorite perennials for cutting in the general garden scheme, knowing that only some of the perennials' display will be sacrificed for vases.

In either case, the soil for the cutting garden should be as nearly perfect as possible. If it is next to the vegetable garden, the good deeds done to prepare the vegetable patch will benefit the cutting flowers. Drainage, fertility, and a nearby source of water all help. If the hose will not reach to the area, then plan for summer mulches to retain soil moisture and to cut down on weeds.

An excellent mulch for the cutting garden as well as the vegetable garden is the accumulation of the grass clippings gleaned from routine lawn mowings. But beware of spreading them too thickly. A few inches at a time will do. Too thick layers of grass clippings become odoriferous and will not decay properly. Lightly work them in to hasten decay. And watch leaf growth. Additional nitrogen may be needed to supplement the nitrogen usurped by the soil bacteria which breaks down the grass clippings.

Here are some of the best flowers to grow for cutting.

ANNUALS

Aster
Bachelor buttons
Calendula
Cockscomb (*Celosia*)
Cosmos
Dahlia
Flossflower (*Ageratum*)
Gladiolus (bulbs)

Marigold
Pincushion flower
   (*Scabiosa*)
Salvia (blue)
Snapdragon
Stock
Sunflower
Zinnia

PERENNIALS

Aster
Astilbe
Baby's breath
Beebalm (*Monarda*)
Bellflower
   (*Campanula*)
Blanket flower
   (*Gaillardia*)
Chrysanthemum
Coneflower
   (*Rudbeckia*)
Delphinium

Iris
Lupine
Peony
Phlox
Poppy
Rose
Shasta daisy
Sneezeweed
   (*Helenium*)
Sunflower (*Helianthus*)
Tickseed (*Coreopsis*)
Yarrow

When cutting flowers, snip them in mid-morning after the dew has dried on the foliage but before the heat of the day. Cut the blooms that are almost but not fully open, as they will last longer. As soon as they are cut, take them indoors and plunge them into a deep bucket of warm, not cold, water. The stems will absorb the moisture more rapidly. Then put the bucket in a cool cellar or garage and arrange the flowers that evening or the next morning. You may like to recut the stems in arranging the design; this also helps the flowers last longer. Change the water frequently and keep the arrangement out of strong sunlight.

Hanging Planters

When there is need for more planting space, hanging planters offer a decorative dimension. They can be hung from trees, from patio awnings, from breezeways, and from porches. Just be sure that the hooks are strong enough to support the weight. When watered, these containers weigh much more than when dry. Hardware stores and garden shops have wide selections of brackets and hooks with instructions for hanging them.

Avoid placing hanging plants where there are high winds or strong heat reflection from other buildings. You will never win the constant battle with the elements.

The simplest hanging planters are the polystyrene pots with three-stranded wire hangers sold at garden centers. Either white or green, they come in sizes from 5 to 10 inches wide. They are usually planted with impatiens, begonias, or petunias and provide a ready color accent.

The fascination with macramé has also expanded hanging-plant possibilities. Assorted shapes and sizes of clay pots can now be hung by slipping them into the decorative macramé nets. The results are imaginative splashes of color to look up to.

The more complicated hanging planters are the wire frame baskets which you have to line with moss and fill yourself. Although they are the most work, they offer the widest range of possibilities for the plants grow out from the center and the top sides of the frame, into a ball of color. The wire baskets are either 12 or 14 inches wide.

To plant the wire basket, soak a package or two of sphagnum moss from the garden center. Wring it out until it is almost dry and spread it into flat pieces. Lay them along the inside bottom and up part of the sides of the basket. You may have to poke the moss into the wire frame a bit to make it secure.

Have waiting on the side a light airy soil mixture. One that works well is 2 parts sterilized soil, 1 part perlite, and 1 part sieved compost. Although this mixture is not highly fertile, it is lightweight and holds moisture well. You will just have to use water soluble fertilizer at quarter rate each week to keep the plants thriving.

Fill the basket about one-third full with the soil mixture, as far as the moss lining goes. Then add more sphagnum moss liner around the frame to fill it to the top. Now you are ready to start setting in the young plants. Those that are in bud and are just starting to bloom will provide fast results.

The plants will be squeezed next to each other root ball by root ball so you may need more than you think. Depending on the plants selected you can easily use two six-packs of seedlings in a 12-inch planter. Petunias are marvelous in hanging planters, either all one color or a mixture. Impatiens does well, too. So do begonias, either the wax bedding begonias or, even better, the pendulous tuberous begonias. But caution, these latter begonias will not tolerate full sun, only the gentle morning sun.

Other good candidates are the trailing plants: sweet alyssum, lobelia, nasturtiums, campanula, vinca, or ivy. These can be mixed with upright growers such as marigolds or dwarf geraniums. The full-sized geraniums take up a lot of space.

To make the hanging planter look full and colorful, insert some of the trailing plants from outside into the soil pocket. Use a screwdriver to tear a hole in the moss liner, then push the root ball through the hole and pull it through to the inside. Then tuck other trailing plants along the edges inside in between the roots of these plants. Save the center for the upright plants and fill in the spaces not taken up by the root ball. Firm them all in well.

Watering will settle in the plants. When it drains away, check to see if there are holes or cavities and fill them in with the soil mixture. Set the planter out of direct sunlight for a day or so just to be sure all is well. Then hang and enjoy it.

Maintenance of hanging planters is fairly routine. They will need to be checked daily, lest they dry out. Remember, they will be exposed to more wind and light than on-the-ground plants. When you water hanging plants, soak them through until water drips off them or into the attached drain saucer. Tilt it slightly to be sure all the excess drains off. And don't forget to feed moss-lined baskets at least once a week. Feed the plastic or clay and terra-cotta pots regularly, too.

Check these plants frequently for dead or browned leaves. Prune them off and don't hesitate to pinch back and prune back overgrown plants when they become too voluptuous.

Pots and Tubs

Huge clay pots, tubs made of redwood, oak barrels, and imported terra-cotta planters provide room for a garden where there seems to be none. They allow flower color on a sunny terrace. Condominium gardeners can fit them on balconies or patios. Vacation-house gardeners can line them up on the deck of the mountain retreat. Homeowners can follow steps and walkways with them to brighten the doorway. Where space is at a premium, containers serve as planting room. Wherever imagination leads, pots, tubs, and movable gardens come into their own.

In theory any plants that can grow in the ground can grow in containers, but in practice only the dwarf or medium height flowers grow well, and, for practicality, you are safest if you grow only annuals. In cold winter climates, perennials would be difficult to carry through, since both the containers and the plants themselves could be damaged in severe weather.

The growing rules change only slightly for plants in containers. Because the root space is confined, the plants will need more frequent watering and feeding. And because they will have this extra-special tending, they can be placed closer together than in the ground.

One problem with containers is that they become very heavy, especially when they are filled with plants and then watered! Any step to lighten the soil first is a help if the containers ever have to be moved to clean the area or make more space.

There are lightweight soilless mixes available at garden centers. They can be used, but with reservations. If many containers have to be planted, this can be costly. Also, these soilless mixes, which are a blend of bark or peat moss plus perlite or vermiculite and slow-release fertilizers, are so lightweight they do not provide a solid anchoring for plant roots. In high winds plants can be pulled right out of their "socks."

More practical is to make your own planting mix of 1 part soil, 1 part perlite or vermiculite, and 1 part fine bark, peat moss, or compost. This heavy-quality mix works well for all container potting. It drains, holds moisture, and provides good root anchoring. Plants growing in it will thrive provided you remember to feed them on a regular basis, at least biweekly, with a water-soluble fertilizer.

As with all container potting, a drainage layer over the essential drain holes is important. This can be whatever is handy—old potsherds, gravel, cat-box filler, or packing "noodles." The lighter the drainage layer, the better. Put a filter over the drainage layer to prevent the soil from running out, either plastic window screening or sphagnum moss.

If you have containers left over from last year's garden, chances are they were stored with the old soil in them. Don't discard this; it is recyclable. A good scheme is to scoop out a third or so of the soil and replace it with some fresh compost, humus, or peat moss that has been wetted through. Then add a generous handful of superphosphate for each 12-inch pot and work this all in together. Then you will be ready to set in this year's plants.

After many years of trial and error in devising unique combinations for pot gardens, my conclusion is to keep them simple. Somehow, one huge pot filled to overflowing with well-grown petunias, geraniums, or marigolds is a much more pleasing statement of color than an assortment, say, of marigolds, ageratum, and geraniums all vying with each other.

The variety of color and design can be better achieved by arranging several pots of flowers in a group. For instance, three smaller pots of golden marigolds could be used to face down one large tub of red geraniums.

Exceptions are upright growing and drooping plants. Alyssum lends itself well to container gardens as it graces itself over pot edges beautifully and keeps blooming all sum-

Seaside gardeners must choose and plant their flower borders carefully.

Browallia is a splendid hanging plant for summer-long flowering.

238

mer long. It is a fine companion for geraniums, ageratum, marigolds, impatiens, zinnias, daisies of all kinds, and begonias.

Here are some spectaculars to try in pots, tubs, and jardinieres: petunias, marigolds, impatiens, geraniums, celosia (the plumy type), coleus, nasturtiums, verbena, begonias, ageratum, and zinnias.

Use your imagination. Often the unexpected flowers can be the most successful and, who knows, you might start a trend. Don't forget the trailing green plants, such as vinca or ivy, that can add some additional glamour to the container garden.

Gardening by the Sea

The ocean breezes may please the beach hounds and surfers, but they are relentless for gardeners. A book could be written on this vast subject, but suffice it to say that seaside garden plants will need all the help they can get from the ground up.

Initially, the soil is the key to success or failure. All soils that border the oceans are sandy, severely lacking in any organic content. This means they are sievelike, so that water and all soil nutrients drain right through them. No wonder sand dunes are so sparse of greenery. Only the toughest beach grasses can survive the meager nutrition and the constant buffeting winds.

The first rule for any seaside garden is add, add, add organic matter. It should be done every year without fail, and in quantity. Seaside gardeners are learning that seaweed washed up freely by the tides is their best source of soil organic matter. The salt residue does not seem to be any problem and gardeners have been using seaweed with excellent results both as a garden mulch and, dug in in the fall or spring, as an enrichment to the soil.

In addition to this natural source, weathered manures, peat moss, and compost derived from kitchen wastes (vegetable matter only) are excellent improvers of seaside soil.

Once the soil has been richly endowed with organic matter, it will retain the nutrients you add in the form of either granular or water-soluble fertilizer. The soil will also be able to retain the much-needed moisture when you or nature provide it.

All seaside gardens benefit from some sort of baffle against the winds. If the garden is to be set directly in the brunt of the salt-water breezes, this windbreak is essential. Try screen plants, such as Japanese black pine, beach plum, or any of the junipers. Or fencing. Good old privet hedge somehow endures the ocean breezes and serves well, but you might choose to be more imaginative.

The flowers that grow best by the sea are those that love the sun most. They have the sunny colors. They survive as long as they are watered well, fed frequently, and watched over carefully. Some do better than others, particularly portulaca, poppies, bachelor buttons, zinnias, marigolds, petunias, cosmos, cleome, snapdragon, verbena, and the like. Sunflowers and strawflowers do very well, as do the plumy celosias and asters, as the yellow virus does not seem as much a problem as with inland gardens.

Many perennials do well at the ocean front, too, except those that are heavy feeders such as peonies and iris, although some experienced gardeners do grow them with little trouble. More reliable are the plants more easily adapted to shallow soils and dry winds such as balloon flower, bellflower, dusty miller, Oriental poppy, phlox, beebalm, chrysanthemum, and especially the Shasta daisy and veronica. Columbine and coral bells will do well, too, if set in sheltered areas near the house where they can be watered more frequently. And, of course, daylilies will establish themselves easily if given the lee side of the house away from the winds.

If the soil is improved and the wind broken, good things can happen in the seaside garden. Experiment and be willing to make some extra effort, and you will be rewarded.

Strawberry Jars

These terra-cotta planters offer a delightful dimension. Their tall, stately posture and open-mouthed pockets invite imagination in planting schemes. The trick is the planting and, after the planting, the carrying, as the large ones are heavy. Once mastered, the real pleasure can follow.

An enterprising gardener solved the strawberry planting jar problem out of necessity. Asked by her garden club to enter a competition for strawberry jars, she had to devise a method that would permit her to carry and haul a large strawberry jar to the show. With ingenuity, Mrs. Charles Mackall, an experienced Connecticut gardener, developed a "sock" method for planting strawberry jars. When fully planted it is lightweight and easy to carry.

Her method involves filling the core of the strawberry jar with perlite, the almost weightless micaceous material used to root cuttings

A short-cut to planting the strawberry jar is to fill it with lightweight perlite first. Then follow Mrs. Grace Mackall's method of soil socks, made of old nylon stockings. These are stuffed into the jar's pockets, the roots of succulents pushed into them, and a large succulent saved for the top.

and lighten potting soils. The roots of the individual plants are tucked into nylon socks of soil stuffed into each pocket.

Before starting to fill the jar, however, be sure to put a piece of broken potsherd or nylon netting over the drainage hole in the bottom of the strawberry jar. Then fill the jar to the level of the first pocket with perlite.

Keep several pairs of old nylons handy. Cut them into 4-inch strips and tie a knot in the bottom of each to make a soil sock. Fill each sock with about a cupful of moistened potting soil.

Then working from the center hole down, the sock is placed at a 45-degree angle on top of the perlite with the open end of the sock extending out of the pocket hole. It will be tucked out of sight when the plants are in place.

Then tuck one seedling in each sock in each pocket. You'll have to gather the roots into a small wad and stuff them tightly into the sock of soil. Any pieces of sock that show can be stuffed back in or cut off if too long. Hairpins can be used to secure the plants if they are wiggly.

When the first tier of pockets is planted, add more perlite to fill the core of the jar to the second tier, insert the socks and plants, and so on until the jar is filled. The top of the strawberry jar is filled with a large spectacular crowning plant such as a geranium.

If any plants die or need to be replaced, all you have to do is yank them out of the soil and the sock can stay in place while a substitute plant is inserted.

For the pockets, you might use some of the trailing annuals such as sweet alyssum and petunias. For the top, marigolds and zinnias do well. In the shade, you can try begonias and lobelia or vinca and ivy as trailing plants.

The strawberry jar is easy to care for. Watering is the most difficult chore. To test to see if it's dry, you can use one of the new moisture meters with the long metal probe. Water from the top down but check the pockets and, if they seem dry, add a little water to each one. Fertilizing is important, too. Feed your strawberry jars with half-strength fertilizer once a month.

Vacation House

There is no need to be without a simple flower garden at the vacation house rented for a month or six weeks. Tubs or simple borders of bright flowers can provide a little summer color and even a few blossoms for cutting. You'll just have to plan ahead.

Where most vacation or summer houses are located, chances are the garden centers are few and far between. And any stock of started seedlings that the plant store might have would be leftovers indeed.

The better course is to buy a few seedlings to take along with you. Select the easy-to-grow annuals such as petunias, impatiens, begonias, ageratum, zinnias, and marigolds. If the plants are strong and in bud, all to the good. Tuck them into the car before leaving. Avoid the trunk if you have a long way to go.

Plant the seedlings as soon as you can and tend them faithfully. If boosted the second week or so with water-soluble fertilizer, which you also remembered to pack in the car along with spade and trowel, you will have flowers to enjoy. A garden at home away from home.

Seeds might be tempting to take along. Unless you plan to occupy the summer home for two months or more, you will be disappointed.

Although most landlords would never fault the desire to brighten their property with flowers, you might check with them before digging up any new garden patch to set in the flowers.

And before leaving when the vacation period is over, check with the new tenants if you can. They may want to relax completely and not be bothered with tending anything—even flowers. Then it is your duty, hard as it may be, to clear the garden when you leave, especially potted or tubbed plants which would not endure neglect.

Window Boxes

A window box provides another opportunity for a garden. How many brownstones, apartments, and even tiny cottages with little land can be brightened by those long rectangular boxes hung carefully under each window! Window boxes will accommodate a surprising number of flowers, and bloom all summer long. For instance, a window box 3 feet long by 2 feet wide by 1 foot deep will hold 24 seedlings.

Ready-made window boxes abound at garden centers. Most of them are of durable redwood, pine, or plastic. Avoid the metal ones, as they rust and deteriorate in no time. Besides, they become very heavy when laden with plants and soil.

Brackets should be sturdy so the window boxes are secure when filled and not easily toppled in wind storms. If the window boxes are over streets or walkways, you will have to be doubly sure that they are securely anchored. Sometimes window boxes are hung along terraces or on balcony railings. These must be bolted fast in metal brackets to be secure.

As with all containers, window boxes must have drainage holes. Most of the ready-made ones will have the holes in them. If not, be sure to drill them before filling them with plants. For the plants are stuffed tightly—root ball by root ball—in window boxes and they will need quick drainage of excess moisture or the roots may rot.

Cover the large drainage holes with shards or put a layer of gravel or packing "noodles" in the bottom. Allow for at least a 1-inch layer. Then cover that layer with plastic wind screening or some sphagnum moss so the soil does not leach through.

Next, add a few inches of lightweight soil mix to the bottom of the window box. You can stretch out the soil with a half-portion of vermiculite or perlite added to the potting soil, which will not only keep the window box light in weight but also aid drainage.

Have all your seedlings at hand when you are ready to plant. Window boxes look best when a selection of three kinds of plants are used: one kind to trail and drape over the front, a second as a middle filler, and a third for height in the back. These plants will be staggered on top of a layer of soil (about half the depth of the box) so they are not lined up one directly in front of the other.

Set the plants in place to your satisfaction before filling in between them with the rest of the soil mix. This is the easiest way to plant a window box, for it allows you to rearrange the seedlings without disturbing their roots. Just be sure that there is enough soil filler in the bottom of the box so that the level of soil around the seedlings will be the same height in the box as it was in their original pots. When the plants are in position, fill in with more soil and tamp firm to anchor the seedlings in place.

Here are some good triplets to consider when planting a window box:

> Red geraniums, flossflower, sweet alyssum
> Pink petunias, flossflower, vinca
> White petunias, golden marigolds, vinca or ivy to trail
> Scarlet sage, coleus, vinca
> Creeping zinnia, browallia, pompon zinnias

Since window-box cultivation is high-intensity gardening you will have to give it high-intensity care. Feeding it is a must. One easy way is to use quarter-rate water-soluble fertilizer weekly. If you follow this regimen, feed the window boxes on the same day every week so you don't overdo it.

The plants must be watched carefully. Pinch off any faded flowers promptly. And if the plants grow too thick and crowd each other, don't hesitate to prune; you may even have to pull out a plant or two.

A window box looks best when it is rather stuffed and full of color. But few plants can thrive if they don't have enough room to stretch their blooms open.

Watering will be as important as feeding. In the heat of the summer, window boxes may need to be watered at least once a day. Some plants are more tolerant of heat than others. Coleus, for instance, is a thin-leaved and very thirsty plant that needs daily attention. Poke your finger deeply into the soil to check. In a few days, you will get the sense of how often the plants need watering.

8. flower lists and useful information

All-America Award Winning
Flower Varieties in General Commerce

Variety	Year of Award
*Alyssum "Pink Heather"	1959
*Alyssum "Rosie O'Day"	1961
*Alyssum "Royal Carpet"	1953
Aster "El Monte"	1936
Aster "Los Angeles"	1934
*Basil "Ornamental Dark Opal"	1962
Calendula "Chrysantha"	1934
*Carnation "Juliet" Hybrid	1975
*Celosia "Fireglow"	1964
*Celosia "Golden Triumph"	1968
*Celosia "Red Fox"	1974
*Celosia "Toreador"	1955
Chrysanthemum "El Dorado"	1934
*Cleome "Pink Queen"	1942
*Columbine "McKana Giant"	1955
Cornflower "Jubilee Gem"	1937
Cosmos "Dazzler"	1943
Cosmos "Diablo"	1974
Cosmos "Radiance"	1948
Cosmos "Sunset"	1966
Cynoglossum "Firmament"	1939
*Dahlia "Redskin"	1975

Variety	Year of Award
*Delphinium "Connecticut Yankee"	1965
*Dianthus "Bravo"	1962
*Dianthus "China Doll" Hybrid	1970
*Dianthus "Magic Charms" Hybrid	1974
*Dianthus "Queen of Hearts" Hybrid	1971
*Dianthus "Snowfire" Hybrid	1978
*Foxglove "Foxy"	1967
*Geranium "Carefree Scarlet" Hybrid	1968
*Geranium "Carefree Deep Salmon" Hybrid	1968
*Geranium "Carefree Bright Pink" Hybrid	1968
*Geranium "Showgirl" Hybrid	1977
*Gloriosa Daisy "Double"	1961
Hibiscus "Southern Belle" Hybrid	1971
Hollyhock "Indian Spring"	1939
*Hollyhock "Majorette"	1976
Hollyhock "Silver Puffs"	1971
Hollyhock "Summer Carnival"	1972
Hunnemannia "Sunlite"	1934
Larkspur "Blue Bell"	1934
Larkspur "Rosamond"	1934
*Lobelia "Rosamund"	1934
Linaria "Fairy Bouquet"	1934
*Marigold "Bolero"	1970
*Marigold "Butterball"	1942
*Marigold, Dwarf Crested French "Janie"	1980
*Marigold "First Lady"	1968
*Marigold "Gold Galore" Hybrid	1972
*Marigold "Golden Jubilee" Hybrid	1967
Marigold "Mammoth Mum"	1944
*Marigold "Happy Face" Hybrid	1973
*Marigold "Naughty Marietta"	1947
*Marigold "Orange Jubilee" Hybrid	1968
*Marigold "Petite Gold"	1958
*Marigold "Petite Orange"	1958
*Marigold "Petite Harmony"	1958
*Marigold "Primrose Lady" Hybrid	1977
*Marigold "Queen Sophia"	1979
*Marigold "Showboat" Hybrid	1974
*Marigold "Spun Gold"	1960

	Variety	Year of Award
	Marigold "Sunkist"	1943
	Marigold "Toreador" Hybrid	1960
*Marigold "Yellow Galore" Hybrid	1977
	Morning Glory "Early Call Rose"	1970
	Morning Glory "Pearly Gates"	1942
	Morning Glory "Scarlet O'Hara"	1939
	Nasturtium "Glorious Gleam Mixture"	1935
	Nasturtium "Golden Gleam"	1933
	Nasturtium "Golden Globe"	1936
	Nasturtium "Scarlet Gleam"	1935
*Nicotiana "Nicki-Red" Hybrid	1979
*Nierembergia "Purple Robe"	1942
*Pansy "Coronation Gold"	1938
*Pansy "Giant Majestic Mixed" Hybrid	1966
*Pansy "Imperial Blue" Hybrid	1975
*Pansy "Majestic White with Blotch" Hybrid	1966
*Pansy "Orange Prince" Hybrid	1979
*Pepper, Ornamental "Holiday Cheer"	1979
*Petunia "Appleblossom" Hybrid	1965
*Petunia "Ballerina"	1952
*Petunia "Blushing Maid" Hybrid	1977
*Petunia "Circus" Hybrid	1972
*Petunia "Colossal Shades of Rose"	1946
*Petunia "Comanche" Hybrid	1953
*Petunia "Coral Satin" Hybrid	1961
*Petunia "Fire Chief"	1950
*Petunia "Glitters" Hybrid	1957
*Petunia "Paleface" Hybrid	1955
*Petunia "Red Satin" Hybrid	1957
*Petunia "Velvet Ball"	1939
*Phlox "Glamour"	1960
*Phlox "Twinkle"	1957
	Scabiosa "Blue Moon"	1939
*Sweet William "Red Monarch"	1966
*Snapdragon "Bright Butterflies" Hybrid	1966
*Snapdragon "Floral Carpet Rose" Hybrid	1965

Variety	Year of Award
*Snapdragon "Little Darling" Hybrid	1971
*Snapdragon "Madame Butterfly" Hybrid	1970
*Snapdragon "Rocket Red," "Orchid," "Rose," "Bronze," "Golden" and "White" Hybrid	1960
Tithonia "Torch"	1951
*Verbena 'Amethyst'	1966
*Verbena "Blaze"	1968
*Verbena "Sangria"	1980
*Vinca "Polka Dot"	1969
Zinnia "Blaze" Hybrid	1954
Zinnia "Bonanza" Hybrid	1964
Zinnia "Carved Ivory" Hybrid	1972
*Zinnia "Cherry Buttons"	1969
Zinnia "Cherry Ruffles" Hybrid	1978
Zinnia "Fantasy Mixed"	1935
Zinnia "Firecracker" Hybrid	1963
Zinnia "Gold Sun" Hybrid	1979
*Zinnia "Old Mexico"	1962
*Zinnia "Persian Carpet"	1952
*Zinnia "Peter Pan Cream" Hybrid	1978
*Zinnia, Compact "Peter Pan Flame" Hybrid	1980
*Zinnia "Peter Pan Gold"	1979
*Zinnia "Peter Pan Pink" Hybrid	1971
*Zinnia "Peter Pan Plum" Hybrid	1971
*Zinnia "Peter Pan Scarlet" Hybrid	1973
*Zinnia "Pink Buttons"	1964
Zinnia "Red Man" Hybrid	1962
Zinnia "Red Sun" Hybrid	1978
Zinnia "Rosy Future"	1969
Zinnia "Scarlet Ruffles" Hybrid	1974
*Zinnia "Thumbelina"	1963
Zinnia "Torch" Hybrid	1969
Zinnia "Wild Cherry" Hybrid	1968
Zinnia "Yelow Ruffles" Hybrid	1978
Zinnia "Yellow Zenith" Hybrid	1965

* Asterisked varieties are especially good as bedding plants.

List of Flower Seed Varieties Awarded by Fleuroselect

1973
Geranium Sprinter
Dianthus Snowflake
Mallow Tanagra

1974
Snapdragon Orange Pixie
Marigold Showboat

1975
Dahlia Redskin
Dianthus Crimson Charm
Dianthus Scarlet Charm
Flower Tobacco Cromson Rock
Marigold Honeycomb
China aster Pinocchio

1976
Zinnia Pink Ruffles
Impatiens Swiss Miss

1977
Strawflower Hot Bikini
Calendula Fiesta Gitana

1978
Alyssum Wonderland
Salvia Victoria
Zinnia Cherry Ruffles
Zinnia Yellow Ruffles

1979
Mallow Silver Cup
Mallow Mont Blanc
Dianthus Crimson Knight
Geranium Red Express
Marigold Orange Boy

Sources for Flower Seeds and Plants

SEEDS

Mail-order catalogues are available from:

Burgess Seed & Plant Company
Galesburg, MI 49053

Burnett Brothers
92 Chambers Street
New York, NY 10007

Burpee Seed Company
Warminster, PA 18991

Comstock, Ferre & Co.
Wethersfield, CT 06109

Gurney Seed and Nursery
  Company
Yankton, SD 57078

Joseph Harris Company
Moreton Farm
Rochester, NY 14624

Herbst Brothers, Seedsmen,
  Inc.
1000 N. Main Street
Brewster, NY 10509

253

Park Seed Company
Greenwood, SC 29647

Thompson & Morgan
Box 100
Farmingdale, NJ 07727

Stokes Seeds, Inc.
Box 548
Buffalo, NY 14240

Seed-rack packets at garden centers:

Ferry-Morse Seed Company

Hart Seed Company

Fredonia Seed Company

Northrup King Company

PLANTS

Mail-order catalogues are available from:

Blackthorne Gardens
48 Quincy Street
Holbrook, MA 02343

   Catalogue $1   Hostas

Bluestone Perennials
7211 Middle Ridge Road
Madison, OH 44057

Carroll Gardens
Westminster, MD 21157

Garden Place
6780 Heisley Road
Mentor, OH 44060

Lamb Nurseries
East 101 Sharp Avenue
Spokane, WA 99202

David Reath
Box 251
Vulvan, MI 49892

   Peonies

Thon's Inc.
4815 Oak Street
Crystal Lake, IL 60014

   Chrysanthemums

Wayside Gardens
Hodges, SC 29695

   Catalogue $1

White Flower Farm
Litchfield, CT 06759

   Catalogue subscription $5

Gilbert H. Wild & Son
Sarcoxie, MO 64862

   Catalogue $1
   Daylilies, Iris, Peonies

Cooperative Extension Services, by State

Alabama
Cooperative Extension Service
Auburn University
Auburn 36830

Arizona
Cooperative Extension Service
University of Arizona
College of Agriculture
Tucson 85721

Arkansas
Cooperative Extension Service
University of Arkansas
P.O. Box 391
Little Rock 72203

California
Agricultural Extension Service
University of California
2200 University Avenue
Berkeley 94720

Colorado
Cooperative Extension Service
Colorado State University
Fort Collins 80523

Connecticut
Cooperative Extension Service
University of Connecticut
College of Agriculture
  and Natural Resources
Storrs 06268

Delaware
Cooperative Extension Service
University of Delaware
College of Agricultural Sciences
Newark 19711

District of Columbia
Cooperative Extension Service
University of D.C.
1331 H Street N.W.
Washington, D.C. 20005

Florida
Cooperative Extension Service
University of Florida
Institute of Food
  and Agricultural Sciences
Gainesville 32611

Georgia
Cooperative Extension Service
University of Georgia
College of Agriculture
Athens 30602

Idaho
Cooperative Extension Service
University of Idaho
College of Agriculture
Moscow 83843

Illinois
Cooperative Extension Service
University of Illinois
College of Agriculture
Urbana 61801

Indiana
Cooperative Extension Service
Purdue University
West Lafayette 47907

Iowa
Cooperative Extension Service
Iowa State University
Ames 50011

Kansas
Cooperative Extension Service
Kansas State University
Manhattan 66506

Kentucky
Cooperative Extension Service
University of Kentucky
College of Agriculture
Lexington 40506

Louisiana
Cooperative Extension Service
State University
A & M College
University Station
Baton Rouge 70803

Maine
Cooperative Extension Service
University of Maine
Orono 04473

Maryland
Cooperative Extension Service
University of Maryland
College Park 20742

Massachusetts
Cooperative Extension Service
University of Massachusetts
Amherst 01002

Michigan
Cooperative Extension Service
Michigan State University
East Lansing 48824

Minnesota
Agricultural Extension Service
University of Minnesota
Institute of Agriculture
St. Paul 55108

Mississippi
Cooperative Extension Service
Mississippi State University
State College 39762

Missouri
Cooperative Extension Service
University of Missouri
Columbia 65211

Montana
Cooperative Extension Service
Montana State University
Bozeman 59715

Nebraska
Cooperative Extension Service
University of Nebraska
College of Agriculture
and Natural Resources
Lincoln 68583

Nevada
Cooperative Extension Service
University of Nevada
College of Agriculture
Reno 89557

New Hampshire
Cooperative Extension Service
University of New Hampshire
College of Life Sciences
and Agriculture
Durham 03824

New Jersey
Cooperative Extension Service
Cook College
Rutgers—The State University
New Brunswick 08903

New Mexico
Cooperative Extension Service
New Mexico State University
Box 3AE, Agriculture Bldg.
Las Cruces 88003

New York
Cooperative Extension Service
Cornell University
State University of New York
Ithaca 14853

North Carolina
Cooperative Extension Service
North Carolina State University
P.O. Box 5157
Raleigh 27607

North Dakota
Cooperative Extension Service
North Dakota State University
    of Agriculture
    and Applied Science
University Station
Fargo 58102

Ohio
Cooperative Extension Service
Ohio State University
Agriculture Administration Bldg.
2120 Fyffe Road
Columbus 43210

Oklahoma
Cooperative Extension Service
Oklahoma State University
139 Agricultural Hall
Stillwater 74074

Oregon
Cooperative Extension Service
Oregon State University
Corvallis 97331

Pennsylvania
Cooperative Extension Service
The Pennsylvania State
    University
College of Agriculture
323 Agricultural
    Administration Bldg.
University Park 16802

Rhode Island
Cooperative Extension Service
University of Rhode Island
Kingston 02881

South Carolina
Cooperative Extension Service
Clemson University
Clemson 29631

South Dakota
Cooperative Extension Service
South Dakota State University
College of Agriculture
Brookings 57007

Tennessee
Agricultural Extension Service
University of Tennessee
Institute of Agriculture
P.O. Box 1071
Knoxville 37901

Texas
Agricultural Extension Service
Texas A & M University
College Station 77843

Utah
Cooperative Extension Service
Utah State University
Logan 84322

Vermont
Cooperative Extension Service
University of Vermont
Burlington 05401

Virginia
Cooperative Extension Service
Virginia Polytechnic Institute
Blacksburg 24061

Washington
Cooperative Extension Service
Washington State University
College of Agriculture
Pullman 99163

West Virginia
Cooperative Extension Service
West Virginia University
Morgantown 26506

Wisconsin
Cooperative Extension Service
University of Wisconsin
432 N. Lake Street
Madison 53706

Wyoming
Agricultural Extension Service
University of Wyoming
College of Agriculture
University Station Box 3354
Laramie 82070

Books to Read

DESIGN AND HISTORY

Camp, Wendall H.; Boswell, Victor R.; and Magness, John R. *The World in Your Garden*. Washington, DC: National Geographic Society, 1957.

Coats, Peter. *Flowers in History*. New York: Viking Press, 1970.

Dietz, Marjorie J. *Landscaping and the Small Garden*. Garden City, NY: Doubleday, 1973.

Fairbrother, Nan. *The Nature of Landscape Design as an Art Form, a Craft, a Social Necessity*. New York: Alfred A. Knopf, 1974.

Grasby, Nancy. *Imaginative Small Gardens*. New York: Hearthside Press, 1963.

Haring, Elda. *Color for Your Yard and Garden*. New York: Hawthorn Books, 1971.

Weber, Nelva M. *How to Plan Your Own Home Landscape*. Indianapolis: Bobbs-Merrill, 1977.

Wright, Richardson. *The Story of Gardening*. New York: Dover Books, 1934.

258

GENERAL

Crockett, James Underwood. *Annuals.* Alexandria, VA: Time-Life Books, 1971.

——. *Perennials.* VA: Alexandria, Time-Life Books, 1971.

Cruso, Thalassa. *Making Things Grow Outdoors.* New York: Alfred A. Knopf, 1971.

Cumming, Roderick W. *The Chrysanthemum Book.* New York: D. Van Nostrand, 1964.

—— and Lee, Robert E. *Contemporary Perennials.* New York: Macmillan, 1960.

Hudak, Joseph. *Gardening with Perennials Month by Month.* New York: Quadrangle, 1976.

Nehrling, Arno and Nehrling, Irene. *The Picture Book of Annuals.* New York: Arco, 1977.

——. *The Picture Book of Perennials.* New York: Atheneum, 1968.

Robbins, Ann Roe. *How to Grow Annuals.* New York: Dover Books, 1977.

Sackville-West, Victoria. *Garden Book.* New York: Atheneum, 1968.

Taylor, Norman. *The Guide to Garden Flowers, Their Identity and Culture.* Boston: Houghton-Mifflin, 1958.

Wilson, Helen Van Pelt. *Successful Gardening with Perennials.* Garden City, NY: Doubleday, 1975.

PEST AND DISEASE CONTROL

Westcott, Cynthia. *The Gardener's Bug Book,* 4th edn. New York: Doubleday, 1973.

Yepson, Roger B. *Organic Plant Protection.* Emmaus, PA: Rodale Press, 1976.

SPECIAL USES

Coon, Nelson. *Gardening for Fragrance Indoors and Out.* New York: Hearthside Press, 1967.

Floyd, Harriet. *Plant It Now, Dry It Later.* New York: McGraw-Hill, 1973.

Foley, Daniel J. *Gardening by the Sea from Coast to Coast.* Radnor, PA: Chilton Books, 1965.

Karel, Leonard. *Dried Flowers from Antiquity to the Present*. Metuchen, NJ: Scarecrow Press, 1973.

Truex, Philip. *The City Gardener*. New York: Alfred A. Knopf, 1964.

Wilson, Helen Van Pelt and Bell, Leonie. *The Fragrant Year, Scented Plants for Your Garden and Your House*. New York: Barrows, 1967.

English-Latin Index of Flowers

ANNUALS

African daisy	*Arctotis stoechadifolia*
Bachelor buttons	*Centaurea cyanus*
Begonia	*Begonia semperflorens*
Browallia	*Browallia americana*
Butterfly flower	*Schizanthus pinnatus*
Calendula	*Calendula officinalis*
China aster	*Callistephus chinensis*
Cockscomb	*Celosia cristata; plumosa*
Coleus	*Coleus x hybridus*
Cosmos	*Cosmos species*
Creeping zinnia	*Santvialia procumbens*
Cup flower	*Nierembergia hippomanica violacea*
Dahlberg daisy	*Dyssodia tenuiloba*
Dahlia	*Dahlia pinnata*
Dusty miller	*Senecio species*
Flossflower	*Ageratum Houstonianum*
Flowering tobacco	*Nicotiana alata*
Four o'clock	*Mirabilis Jalapa*
Gazania	*Gazania ringens*
Geranium	*Pelargonium hortorum hybrids*
Heliotrope	*Heliotropium arborescens*
Impatiens	*Impatiens Wallerana*
Lobelia	*Lobelia Erinus*
Love in a mist	*Nigella damascena*
Marigold	*Tagetes species*
Mexican sunflower	*Tithonia rotundifolia*
Mignonette	*Reseda odorata*
Moss rose	*Portulaca grandiflora*

Nasturtium	*Tropaeolum majus*
Painted tongue	*Salpiglossis sinuata*
Pansy	*Viola x Wittrockiana*
Periwinkle	*Catharanthus roseus*
Petunia	*Petunia x hybrida*
Phlox	*Phlox Drummondii*
Pincushion flower	*Scabiosa atropurpurea*
Pinks	*Dianthus chinensis v. Heddewigii*
Poppy	*Papaver species*
Salvia	*Salvia species*
Snapdragon	*Antirrhinum majus*
Spider flower	*Cleome Hasslerana*
Stock	*Matthiola incana*
Strawflower	*Helichrysum bracteatum*
Sunflower	*Helianthus annuus*
Swan River daisy	*Brachycome iberidifolia*
Sweet alyssum	*Lobularia maritima*
Sweet pea	*Lathyrus odoratus*
Tahoka daisy	*Machaeranthera tanacetifolia*
Verbena	*Verbena x hybrida*
Wishbone flower	*Torenia Fournieri*
Zinnia	*Zinna elegans*

PERENNIALS

Alkanet	*Anchusa azurea*
Aster	*Aster species*
Astilbe	*Astilbe species*
Avens	*Geum Quellyon*
Baby's breath	*Gypsophila paniculata*
Balloon flower	*Platycodon grandiflorus*
Basket of gold	*Aurinia saxatilis*
Beardtongue	*Penstemon barbatus*
Beebalm	*Monarda didyma*
Bellflower	*Campanula species*
Blanket flower	*Gaillardia x grandiflora*
Bleeding heart	*Dicentra spectabilis*
Candytuft	*Iberis sempervirens*
Christmas rose	*Helleborus niger*
Chrysanthemum	*Chrysanthemum species*
Columbine	*Aquilegia x hybrida*
Coneflower	*Rudbeckia fulgida*

Coral bells	*Heuchera sanguinea*
Daylily	*Hemerocallis species*
Delphinium	*Delphinium elatum*
Evening primrose	*Oenothera fruticosa*
False dragonhead	*Physostegia virginiana*
Flax	*Linum perenne*
Forget-me-not	*Myosotis scorpioides*
Foxglove	*Digitalis purpurea*
Gas plant	*Dictamnus albus*
Geranium	*Geranium species*
Golden Marguerite	*Anthemis tinctoria*
Hollyhock	*Alcea rosea*
Iris	*Iris species*
Leopards-bane	*Doronicum cordatum*
Loosestrife	*Lythrum Salicaria*
Lupine	*Lupinus polphyllus*
Monkshood	*Aconitum Napellus*
Mountain bluet	*Centaurea montana*
Oriental poppy	*Papaver orientale*
Peony	*Paeonia lactiflora*
Phlox	*Phlox species*
Pinks	*Dianthus species*
Plantain lily	*Hosta species*
Primroses	*Primula species*
Rock cress	*Arabis caucasica*
Sea pink	*Armeria maritima*
Sneezeweed	*Helenium autumnale*
Speedwell	*Veronica species*
Stokes' aster	*Stokesia laevis*
Sunflower	*Helianthus decapetalus v. multiflorus*
Tickseed	*Coreopsis lanceolata*
Tufted pansy	*Viola cornuta*
Yarrow	*Achillea species*

Latin-English Index of Flowers

ANNUALS

Ageratum Houstonianum	Flossflower
Antirrhinum majus	Snapdragon
Arctotis stoechadifolia	African daisy

Begonia semperflorens	Begonia
Brachycome iberidifolia	Swan River daisy
Browallia americana	Browallia
Calendula officinalis	Calendula
Callistephus chinensis	China aster
Catharanthus roseus	Periwinkle
Celosia cristata; plumosa	Cockscomb
Centaurea cyanus	Bachelor buttons
Cleome Hasslerana	Spider flower
Coleus x hybridus	Coleus
Cosmos species	Cosmos
Dahlia pinnata	Dahlia
Dianthus chinensis v. Heddewigii	Pinks
Dyssodia tenuiloba	Dahlberg daisy
Gazania ringens	Gazania
Helianthus annuus	Sunflower
Helichrysum bracteatum	Strawflower
Heliotropium arborescens	Heliotrope
Impatiens Wallerana	Impatiens
Lathyrus odoratus	Sweet pea
Lobelia Erinus	Lobelia
Lobularia maritima	Sweet alyssum
Machaeranthera tanacetifolia	Tahoka daisy
Matthiola incana	Stock
Mirabilis Jalapa	Four o'clock
Nicotiana alata	Flowering tobacco
Nierembergia hippomanica violacea	Cup flower
Nigella damascena	Love in a mist
Papaver species	Poppy
Pelargonium hortorum hybrids	Geranium
Petunia x hybrida	Petunia
Phlox Drummondii	Phlox
Portulaca grandiflora	Moss rose
Reseda odorata	Mignonette
Salpiglossis sinuata	Painted tongue
Salvia species	Salvia
Sanvitalia procumbens	Creeping zinnia
Scabiosa atropurpurea	Pincushion flower
Schizanthus pinnatus	Butterfly flower
Senecio species	Dusty miller

Tagetes species	Marigold
Tithonia rotundifolia	Mexican sunflower
Torenia Fournieri	Wishbone flower
Tropaeolum majus	Nasturtium
Verbena x hybrida	Pansy
Viola x Wittrockiana	Verbena
Zinnia elegans	Zinnia

PERENNIALS

Achillea species	Yarrow
Aconitum Napellus	Monkshood
Alcea rosea	Hollyhock
Anchusa azurea	Alkanet
Anthemis tinctoria	Golden Marguerite
Aquilegia x hybrida	Columbine
Arabis caucasica	Rock cress
Armeria maritima	Sea pink
Aster species	Aster
Astilbe species	Astilbe
Aurinia saxatilis	Basket of gold
Campanula species	Bellflower
Centaurea montana	Mountain bluet
Chrysanthemum species	Chrysanthemum
Coreopsis lanceolata	Tickseed
Delphinium elatum	Delphinium
Dianthus species	Pinks
Dicentra spectabilis	Bleeding heart
Dictamnus albus	Gas plant
Digitalis purpurea	Foxglove
Doronicum cordatum	Leopards-bane
Gaillardia x grandiflora	Blanket flower
Geranium species	Geranium
Geum Quellyon	Avens
Gypsophila paniculata	Baby's breath
Helenium autumnale	Sneezeweed
Helianthus decapetalus v. multiflorus	Sunflower
Helleborus niger	Christmas rose
Hemerocallis species	Daylily
Heuchera sanguinea	Coral bells
Hosta species	Plantain lily
Iberis sempervirens	Candytuft

264

Iris species	Iris
Linum perenne	Flax
Lupinus polphyllus	Lupine
Lythrum Salicaria	Loosestrife
Monarda didyma	Beebalm
Myosotis scorpioides	Forget-me-not
Oenothera fruticosa	Evening primrose
Paeonia lactiflora	Peony
Papaver orientale	Oriental poppy
Penstemon barbatus	Beardtongue
Phlox species	Phlox
Physostegia virginiana	False dragonhead
Platycodon grandiflorus	Balloon flower
Primula species	Primroses
Rudbeckia fulgida	Coneflower
Stokesia laevis	Stokes' aster
Veronica species	Speedwell
Viola cornuta	Tufted pansy

index

Page numbers in **boldface** refer to the full description of the plant and its culture. Page numbers in *italics* refer to separate illustrations.

Abelia, 218
Achillea species. *See* Yarrow
Aconitum Napellus. *See* Monkshood
Aegopodium. *See* Goutweed
Ageratum, 11, 37, 46, 51, 102, 143, 221, 230, 245. *See also* Flossflower
Air pollution, 122, 136, 137, 226, 231
Ajuga. *See* Bugle
Alcea rosea. *See* Hollyhock
Alkanet (*Anchusa azurea*), 47, 93, **158**
All-America Selections (AAS), 19, 21–22, 249–52
Alyssum, 11, 37, 51, 52, 221, 238. *See also* Sweet alyssum
Anchusa azurea. *See* Alkanet
Annuals, 5, 7, 27, 30
  in borders, 33, 38–39, *39–41, 42–43*
  "reseeding" of, 5
  from seed, 5, 52, 72, 80, 86
  See also Nurseries and suppliers; indiv. species
Antirrhinum majus. *See* Snapdragon
Aphids, 98, 100, 134, 136, 138, 151, 173
Aquilegia. *See* Columbine
Arabis caucasica. *See* Rock cress

Arctotis grandis. *See* Daisy, blue-eyed
Arctotis stoechadifolia. *See* Daisy, African
Armeria maritima. *See* Sea pink
Artemisia, *219*
Asarum. *See* Ginger
Asperula. *See* Sweet woodruff
Aster (*Aster species*), 11, *15*, 30, 78, 79, 84, 87–88, 92, 94, 100, 152, **159**, 195, 208, 220, 233, 241
  China (*Callistephus chinensis*), **112**
  A. Frikarti, 13, *42*
  Stokes' (*Stokesia laevis*), **207**
Astilbe (*Astilbe species*), 30, 42, 46, 47, 48, 87–88, **160**, *215, 219*, 220, 233
Aurinia saxatilis. *See* Basket of gold
Avens (*Geum Quellyon*), 52, **161**
Azalea, 214, 218, 222

Baby's breath (*Gypsophila paniculata*), 37, 47, 48, **162**, 195, 233
  Bristol Fairy, 13
Bachelor buttons (*Centaurea cyanus*), 46, 47, 48, 92, **107**, 233, 241

267

Balloon flower (*Platycodon grandi-florus*), 47, 56, 77, 87, 92, **163**, 220, 242

Barrenwort (*Epimedium*), 220

Basket of gold (*Aurinia saxatilis*), 48, **164**

Beardtongue (*Penstemon barbatus*), 56, **165**

Bedding plants, 51, 82, 90

Beebalm (*Monarda didyma*), 42, 47, **166**, 221, 233, 242

Beetles, 98, 101

Begonia (*Begonia semperflorens*), 11, 37, 39, 46, 47, 51, 56, 82, 89, **108**, 221, 230, 234, 235, 244, 245
 hybrids, 27
 tuberous, 12

Bellflower (*Campanula species*), 46, 47, 48, 52, **167**, 220, 233, 235, 242

Biennials, 6–7

Black spot, 178

Blackmore and Langdon, 12

Blanket flower (*Gaillardia x grandiflora*), 47, 48, 52, **168**, 230, 233

Bleeding heart (*Dicentra spectabilis*), 30, 47, 87, **169**, 220

Bloodroot, 30

Borders, 30, 31, 37, 38–39, 39–45, 51, 69, 70, 239
 height factor, 34
 planning of, 33–34, 37

Borers, 101, 189

Botrytis, 92, 94, 100, 138, 197

Brachycome iberidifolia. See Daisy, Swan River

Bristol Nursery, 13

Browallia (*Browallia species*), 46, 56, **109**, 248

Bulbs, 27, 30, 33, 41, 42, 77, 78, 104, 218, 222, 223, 230

Bugle (*Ajuga*), 220

Bunchberry (*Cornus canadensis*), 220

Burpee Seed Company, 14

Butterfly flower (*Schizanthus pinnatus*), **110**

Calliopsis (*Coreopsis tinctoria*), **209**

Callistephus chinensis. See Aster, China

Campanula species. See Bellflower; Canterbury bells

Candytuft (*Iberis sempervirens*), 27, 31, 46, **170**, 220, 230

Canterbury bells (*Campanula medium*), 7, 92, 93, **167**

Cardinal flower, 48

Carnations. *See* Pinks

Caterpillars, 95, 98

Catharanthus roseus. See Periwinkle

Celosia cristata, C. plumosa. See Cockscomb

Centaurea cyanus. See Bachelor buttons

Centaurea montana. See Mountain bluet

Chlorosis, 85, 87

Christmas rose (*Hellborus niger*), **171**

Chrysanthemum (*Chrysanthemum species*), 11, 12, 30, 33, 41, 79, 80, 83, 87, 92, 100, **172–73**, 233, 242

Chrysogonum. See Golden star

City gardens and terraces, 25, 49, 81, 83, 90, 225–31

Cleome Hasslerana. See Spider flower

Cockscomb (*Celosia cristata, C. plumosa*), 11, 46, 48, 100, **113**, 233, 241

Coleus (*Coleus species*), 5, 27, 46, 51, 56, 89, 102, *215*, 221, 248

Columbine (*Aquilegia x hybrida*), 17, 22, 52, 56, 100, 101, **174**, 220, 230, 242

Compost, composting, 67, 92, 112, 221, 229, 241

Coneflower (*Rudbeckia fulgida*), 30, 47, 52, 92, **175**, 233
 purple coneflower (*Echinacea purpurea*), **175**

Cooperative extension services, 255–58

Coral bells (*Heuchera sanguinea*), *31*, 46, 47, 48, 56, 87–88, 92, **176**, 220, 230, 242

Coreopsis lanceolata. See Tickseed

Coreopsis tinctoria. See Calliopsis
Cornus canadensis. See Bunchberry
Cosmos (Cosmos bipinnatus, C. sul-
    phureus), 39, 48, 92, **115**, 233, 241
Cranesbills. See Geranium species
Crocus, 30, 218
Crown, 71, 71
Crown rot, 93, 100, 178, 195
Cultivars, 13
Cup flower (Nierembergia hippomanica
    violacea), 46, **116**
Cutting garden, 231–33
Cuttings, 89–90

Daffodils, 30, 42, 218
Dahlia (Dahlia pinnata), 62, 84, 92, 101,
    118, 233
  Coltness, **118**
  Pompons, **118**
  Redskin, 22, **118**
  Unwin Hybrids, **118**
Daisy, 35, 84
  African (Arctotis stoechadifolia), **106**
  blue-eyed (Arctotis grandis), 106
  Dahlberg (Dyssodia tenuiloba), 106
  English, 46
  gloriosa (Rudbeckia hirta), 175
  golden marguerite (Anthemis tinc-
      toria), 52, **186**
  leopard's-bane (Doronicum corda-
      tum), 30, 48, **190**, 221
  Shasta, 30, 42, 48, 87–88, 92, 233, 242
  Swan River (Brachycome iberidifolia),
      149
  Tahoka (Machaeranthera tanacetifo-
      lia), **152**
Damping-off, 56
Daylily (Hemerocallis species), 30, 47,
    50, 71, 102, **177**, 220, 222
Delphinium (Delphinium elatum), 11,
    12, 22, 30, 52, 71, 83, 84, 84, 92,
    93, 100, **178**, 233
Dianthus species. See Pinks

Dicentra spectabilis. See Bleeding heart
Dictamnus albus. See Gas plant
Digitalis purpurea. See Foxglove
Doronicum cordatum. See Daisy, leop-
    ard's-bane
Drainage, 25, 68, 80, 229–30
Dried flowers, 90–91, 231
Dusty miller (Senecio species), 27, 56,
    119, 143, 242
Dutchman's breeches, 169
Dyssodia tenuiloba. See Daisy, Dahl-
    berg

Echinacea purpurea. See Coneflower,
    purple
Epimedium. See Barrenwort
Evening primrose (Oenothera fruticosa),
    47, 52, **179**

Fairbrother, Nan, Nature of Landscape
    Design, The, 34
False dragonhead (Physostegia virgini-
    ana), **180**
False, white hellebore (Veratrum vi-
    ride), 171
Ferns, 214, 218, 222, 223
Fertilizer, 61, 68, 78, 82–83, 222, 223,
    229, 241, 248
Feverfew, 31
Flax (Linum perenne), 47, 48, 52, 87,
    181
Fleuroselect winners, 22, 252
Flossflower (Ageratum Houstonianum),
    31, 42, 46, 56, **120**, 233, 248
Flowering tobacco (Nicotiana alata), 46,
    47, 56, **121**, 221, 230
Fluorescent lights, 51, 55, 61, 62, 63–64
Forget-me-not (Myosotis scorpioides),
    30, 48, 52, **182**, 220

Four o'clock (*Mirabilis Jalapa*), **122**
Foxglove (*Digitalis purpurea*), 6, 22, 56,
    84, 93, **183**, 220
Fungus, 56, 76, 77, 98, 124, 138, 178,
    223. *See also* specific diseases

Gaillardia x grandiflora. See Blanket
    flower
Garden care, 76–102
Garden design and planning, 23–48
    climate, 25–26, 37
    color, 26–27, 37
    drainage, 25, 68
    exposure in, 25
    half-shade in, 24
    hardiness zones, 26
    light in, 24–25, 39, 42–43
    lists and charts, 28–29, 46–48
    shade in, 25, 39, 42–43, 213–24
    soil quality, 25
    succession of bloom, 27, 28–29
    See also Borders; City gardens
Gas plant (*Dictamnus albus*), 37, 47,
    184
Gazania (*Gazania ringens*), **123**
Geranium (*Geranium species*), 11, 33,
    36, 37, 39, 46, 47, 48, 51, 89, 89,
    90, 90, 100, 102, **185**, 221, 230,
    235, 244, 248
    G. dalmaticum, **185**
    G. ibericum, **185**
    G. sanguineum, **185**
Geranium (*Pelargonium hortorum* hy-
    brids), **124**
Geum Quellyon. See Avens
Ginger (*Asarum*), 220
Gladiolus, 233
Golden fleece. *See* Daisy, Dahlberg
Golden marguerite. *See* Daisy
Golden star (*Chrysogonum*), 221
Goutweed (*Aegopodium*), 220
Groundcovers, 136, 153, 185, 199, 214,
    220
Gypsophila paniculata. See Baby's
    breath

Hardiness zones, 26
Haring, Elda, 44–45
Heaving up, 77–78, 93
Helenium autumnale. See Sneezeweed
Helianthus species. See Sunflower
Helichrysum bracteatum. See Straw-
    flower
Heliotrope (*Heliotrope arborescens,
    Valerian officinalis*), 47, **125**
Helleborus niger. See Christmas rose
Helleborus orientalis. See Lenten rose
Hemerocallis species. See Daylily
Hepatica, 30, 220
Heuchera sanguinea. See Coral bells
Hollyhock (*Alcea rosea*), 7, 36, 53, 100,
    102, **187**
Horse mint. *See* Beebalm
Hosta species. See Plantain lily
Hybrids, hybridists, 7–8, 9
    See also Nurseries and suppliers;
    indiv. species

Iberis sempervirens. See Candytuft
Impatiens (*Impatiens Wallerana*), 11,
    26, 39, 46, 47, 51, 56, 79, 82, 89,
    90, 102, **126–27**, 215, 216, 219,
    221, 230, 234, 235, 245
    hybrids, **127**
Ingwerson Nursery, 12
Insecticides. *See* Pesticides
Insects, 76, 77, 94, 95
    See also indiv. species and problems
Iris (*Iris species*), 6, 27, 30, 46, 47, 87,
    101, 102, **188–89**, 232, 233, 241
Iris borer, 101, 189
Ivy, 214, 230, 235, 245, 248

Lamium, 220
Lantana, 37, 230
Larkspur, 46, 100
Lathyrus odoratus. See Sweet pea

Laurel, 214, 218
Lavender, 47, 48
Leafhoppers, 98, 112, 173
Leaf miners, 98, 101, 174
Leaf spots, 100, 173
Lenten rose (*Helleborus orientalis*), **171**
Leopards-bane (*Doronicum cordatum*), 30, 48, **190**, 221
Lily turf (*Liriope*), 221
"Liner" plants, 18
Linnaeus, Carolus, 3–4
Linum perenne. See Flax
Liriope. See Lily turf
Lobelia (*Lobelia Erinus*), 37, 39, 46, 48, 56, **128**, 221, 235, 245
Lobularia maritima. See Sweet alyssum
Loosestrife (*Lythrum Salicaria*), 48, 92, **191**
Love in a mist (*Nigella damascena*), 46, **129**
Lupine (*Lupinus polyphyllus*), 47, 53, **192**, 233
  Russell lupine, 11, 13
Lupinus polyphyllus. See Lupine
Lythrum Salicaria. See Loosestrife

Machaeranthera tanacetifolia. See Daisy, Tahoka
Marigolds (*Tagetes species*), 5, 11, 21, 37, 39, 46, 47, 48, 51, *51*, 52, 71, 82, 92, 100, 101, **130**, 152, 230, 233, 235, 241, 244, 245, 248
  dwarf, 39, 46, 107, **130**
  Nugget Hybrid, 14, *15*
  Showboat, 22
  triploids, **130**
Matthiola incana. See Stock
Mealybugs, 102

Mentha. See Mint
Mertensia. See Virginia bluebell
Michaelmas daisy. See Aster
Mignonette (*Reseda odorata*), 47, **132**

Mildew, 81, 92, 94, 98, 100, 155, 159, 173, 178, 199, 208, 222
Mint (*Mentha*), 220
Mirabilis Jalapa. See Four o'clock
Mites, 98, 102
Monarda didyma. See Beebalm
Monkshood (*Aconitum Napellus*), **193**, 221
Moss rose (*Portulaca grandiflora*), 46, 48, **133**, 241
Mountain bluet (*Centaurea montana*), 48, 53, **194**
Mulch, 5, 77, 78, 80, 84–87, 92, 93, 100, 223, 232
Myosotis scorpioides. See Forget-me-not
Myrtle, 214

Nasturtium (*Tropaeolum majus*), 46, 47, 48, 101, **134**, 235
Nicotiana alata. See Flowering tobacco
Nierembergia hippomanica violacea. See Cup flower
Nigella damascena. See Love in a mist
Nurseries and suppliers, 7–8, 11–14, 17–22, 90, 94, 253–54
  AAS winners, 19, 21–22, 249–52
  Fleuroselect winners, 22, 252
  See also indiv. species

Oconee bells (*Shortia*), 220
Oenothera fruticosa. See Evening primrose
Oswego tea. See Beebalm

Pachysandra, 214
Paeonia lactiflora. See Peony
Paeonia suffruticosa. See Peony, tree
Painted tongue (*Salpiglossis sinuata*), **135**

Pansy (*Viola x Wittrockiana*), 11, 46, 47, 51, 62, 71, 81, 82, **136**, 221
  tufted (*Viola cornuta*), 53, **210**, 221
Papaver species. See Poppy
Park Seed Company, 14, 17
Peat moss, 57, 59, 67, 221, 229, 241
Pelargonium hortorum. See Geranium
Penstemon barbatus. See Beardtongue
Peony (*Paeonia lactiflora*), 6, 12, 30, 37, 47, 50, 78, 80, *80*, 83, 84, 87, 94, 100, **196–97**, 221, 232, 233, 234, 235, 241
  tree peony (*P. suffruticosa*), 197
Perennials, 5–6, 7, 8, 27, 30, 38, 46, 47, 48, 70, 71–72, 80
  in borders, 33–34, 38, 40, *42–43*, *44–45*, 69
  dividing of, 87–89
  propagation of, 6
  from seed, 6, 52
  See also Nurseries and suppliers; indiv. species
Periwinkle (*Catharanthus roseus*), 46, **137**, 221, 230, 235, 245, 248
Perlite, 57, 89, 237, 242, 244
Pesticides, 95–102
  organic, 95
Petunia (*Petunia x hybrida*), 2, 5, 8, 10, 11, 21, 27, 32, 33, *33*, 36, 37, 42, 46, 47, 51, 56, 62, *62*, 72, 81, 85, **138**, 230, 241, 244, 245
  California Giants, 8
  Comanche, 8, 10, 13
  grandiflora, gradiflora double, 8
Phlox (*Phlox species*), 30, *31*, 46, 48, 50, 78, 81, 87–88, 100, 102, 195, **198–99**, 219, 220, 221, 230, 233, 242
  P. divaricata (wild sweet william), **199**
  P. Drummondii, **139**
  P. paniculata (summer phlox), **199**
  P. stolonifera (groundcover), **199**
  P. subulata (moss pink), **199**

Physostegia virginiana. See False dragonhead
Pinching, pinching back, 62, 78, *79, 79*
Pincushion flower (*Scabiosa atropurpurea*), 46, **140**, 233
Pink (*Dianthus species*), 11, 24, 46, 47, 48, 53, 67, 92, **141**, **200**
  Alwoodii Hybrids, **200**
  D. barbatus (sweet william), **141**
  D. carophyllus (carnation), **200**
  D. chinensis, **141**
  D. deltoides (maiden pink), **200**
  D. plumarius (cottage pink), **200**
Plantain lily (*Hosta species*), 27, 46, 47, 48, 71, **201**, *216*, 220, 222
Planters and tubs, 30, 32, 33, 83, 90, 226–30, 234–38, 239, 240, *243*
  See also Window boxes
Platycodon grandiflorus. See Balloon flower
Poppy (*Papaver species*), 233, 241
  Iceland (*P. nudicaule*), 46, **142**
  oriental (*P. orientale*), 30, 87, 93, **195**, 242
  Shirley (*P. rhoeas*), 46, **142**
Portulaca grandiflora. See Moss rose
Primrose (*Primula species*), 47, 48, 53, 56, **202**, 210, 221
  P. japonica, **202**
  P. vulgaris, **202**
Primula species. See Primrose

Red spider mites, 102
Red spiders, 202
Reseda odorata. See Mignonette
Rhizomes, 6
Rhododendron, 214, 218, 222
Rock cress (*Arabis caucasica*), 53, 56, **203**
  Flore Pleno (double), **203**
Roses, 30, 232, 233
Rudbeckia fulgida. See Coneflower
Rudbeckia hirta. See Daisy, gloriosa

Rust (disease), 100, 173

Sackville-West, Victoria, *Garden Book*, 38
Salpiglossis sinuata. See Painted tongue
Salvia (*Salvia species*), 11, 46, 51, 56
  blue salvia (*S. farinacea*), **143**, 233
  scarlet sage (*S. splendens*), 48, **143**
Sanvitalia procumbens. See Zinnia, creeping
Scabiosa atropurpurea. See Pincushion flower
Schizanthus pinnatus. See Butterfly flower
Sea pink (*Armeria maritima*), **204**
Seaside gardens, *239*, 240–41
Sea thrift, 27
Sedums, 221
Seedlings, 49–64, *53*, 72–73, 102
  annuals, 5, 52, 72, 80, 86
  germination of, 54–56, 60–61, 64
  perennials, 6, 52
  unwanted, 82
Senecio cineraria, S. vira-vira. See Dusty miller
Shade, gardening in, 25, *39*, 42–*43*, 213–24
  deep shade, 214
  full shade, 217, 220
  half-shade, 24, 217, 220–21
  light shade, 217–18, 220–21
Shortia. See Oconee bells
Slugs, 102, 138, 171, 177, 178, 201
Snapdragon (*Antirrhinum majus*), 5, 11, *31*, *35*, *39*, 56, 62, 71, 79, 81, 84, 100, 102, **144**, 233, 241
  Rocket, *42*
Sneezeweed (*Helenium autumnale*), 47, 87–88, **205**, 233
Soil preparation and planting, 65–75
  for seaside gardens, 240–41
  for shade, 221–24
  tools, *73*, *74*, *75*
  See also indiv. species

Speedwell (*Veronica species*), 46, 47, 78, 92, **206**, 221, 242
  V. incana, **206**
  V. latifolia, **206**
  V. longifolia subsessilis, **206**
  V. spicata (Blue Peter), **206**
Spider flower (*Cleome Hasslerana*), 47, 48, **145**, 241
Spider mites, 136, 173
Squirrel corn, 169
Staking, 83–84
Stock (*Matthiola incana*), 47, **146**, 233
Strawberry jars, 242–44
Strawflower (*Helichrysum bracteatum*), 56, 92, **147**, 241
Sundrop (*Oenothera* family), **179**
Sunflower (*Helianthus annuus*), 47, 48, 92, **148**, 233, 241
  H. decapetalus v. multiflorus, **208**
  Mexican sunflower (*Tithonia rotundifolia*), **131**
Sweet alyssum (*Lobularia maritima*), 33, 46, 47, 107, 143, **150**, 230, 235, 244, 248
  See also Alyssum
Sweet pea (*Lathyrus odoratus*), 47, 48, **151**
Sweet william, 7, 199
  wild (*Dianthus barbatus*), 141
Sweet woodruff (*Asperula*), 221

Tagetes species. See Marigold
Thinning out, 6
Thrift. *See* Sea pink
Thrips, 98, 102
Tickseed (*Coreopsis lanceolata*), 30, 47, 48, 53, 84, **209**, 233
Tithonia rotundifolia. See Sunflower, Mexican
Tools, *73*, *74*, *75*, *77*
Torenia Fournieri. See Wishbone flower
Trillium, 30, 220
Triploid hybrids, 13–14

Tropaeolum majus. See Nasturtium
Truex, Philip, *City Gardener, The,* 229
Tulips, 30, 42, 218

Valerian officinalis. See Heliotrope
Veratrum viride. See False hellebore
Verbena (*Verbena x hybrida*), 11, 46, 51, **153**, 230, 241
Vermiculite, 57, 59, 89, 229, 237
Vinca. *See* Periwinkle
Viola species. See Pansy
Virginia bluebell (*Mertensia*), 48, 220

Watering, 60–61, 80–81, 88–89, 224, 248
White fly, 102, 120, 230
Wilt disease, 112
Windbreaks, 25, 83, 241
Window boxes, 30, 49, 90, *216,* 247-48
    See also Planters and tubs

Winter rot, 93
Wishbone flower (*Torenia Fournieri*), 46, 48, **154**, 220, 221

Yarrow (*Achillea species*), 12, 27, 48, 56, **211**, 233
    A. filipendulina, **211**
    A. ptarmica, **211**
Yellows (disease), 94, 100, 112, 241

Zinnia (*Zinnia elegans*), 11, 21, *35,* 46, 48, 51, 52, 71, 79, 81, 92, 94, 100, 101, **155**, 230, 233, 241, 244, 245, 248
Cherry Ruffles, 22
creeping (*Sanvitalia procumbens*), 46, 48, **116**, 248
Yellow Ruffles, 22